WHAT KIND OF LOVE IS THIS!

A Story of Adoption Reconciliation

Sandra Kay Musser

Jan Publications
Oaklyn, New Jersey
08107

Dedicated to:

WAYNE
    who decorated my life

               and

MY CHILDREN
    who have filled my life with
    excitement
    exhiliration
    exhaustion
        and grandchildren!

This is a true story. However, some of the names, places, and circumstances have been disguised to protect the privacy of those involved.

Cover design graciously donated by

Jan Urbsaitis
c/o Sun Advertising
68 Seminole Road
Lakewood, New Jersey

What Kind Of Love Is This
Copyright© 1982 by Sandra Kay Musser
All Rights Reserved
Printed in the United States of America
International Standard Book Number: 0-934896-43-7
Library of Congress Catalog Card Number: 82-84236
Jan Publications
Oaklyn, New Jersey 08107

Acknowledgements

It is impossible to acknowledge all those who have played an important part in my life over the past several years. However, I would like to thank a few of them.

Dotti Farrell, Gladys Holiny and Mary Johnson, with whom I worked for ten years, listened for hours as I shared my adoption experience. Not only did they listen, but they laughed and cried with me as well.

Elaine Noll and Anne McCrory, two of my dearest "theological" buddies, with whom I've shared my heart and soul. Their continued moral support has not gone by unnoticed.

There are so many in the movement whom I've come to know and love. Their names would fill the pages of this book. So for now, I especially want to thank those groups who invited me to speak and opened their homes as well as their hearts - The Adoptees' Birthright Committee in Louisiana; Always in Me in Orchard Park, New York; Reunite in Ohio; Orphan Voyage in Florida; the CUB gals in Ohio; the gals connected with Luthern Social Services and the Council on Adoptable Children when they invited me to share at their annual adoptive parents' banquet.

A note of appreciation to the 700 Club Team in Virginia Beach, Virginia, PTL in Charlotte, North Carolina, Hour Magazine in Hollywood, California, as well as several local talk shows around the country, for giving me the opportunity to discuss adoption issues and concerns from a birthparent perspective.

Thanks to Sandie Rocco and Bert Coia for working so closely with me on this manuscript.

A special tribute to Ron Buchman who gave many birthparents and adoptees an invaluable gift - peace of mind.

To Diana Brown, Sally File, Carole Gustavson, Jan Hennessey, Char & Dave Justice, Penny Partridge, Mary Jo Rillera, Emma May Vilardi, Jeanne Strauss, Julie & Ray Bissey, and the entire New Jersey CUB group, a very heartfelt thanks for your extended emotional support and for walking that extra mile.

Thanks to my special family members - Betty & Tom Verica, my sister and brother-in-law; and General Stanton Musser and his wife Dawn, for listening to my heartcries and trying to understand the depth of my hurt; to Sharon and Karen, my half-sisters; to Martha, my step-mother; and West, my step-father, for all their loving support. Especially to Terry, with whom I share a special bond.

To Colleen Martin - how do I say thanks for planting the seed that will bring in the harvest?

Finally, a sincere note of love and appreciation to my daughter for allowing me to share our personal letters and thoughts so that others might benefit from our struggle.

Table of Contents

Dedication..i
Acknowledgements..................................iii
Preface 1
Introduction 3

Section I — Autobiography
      What Kind of Love Is This (Poem)

    Reflections — April, 1982........................7
    The Rest of the Story 9
    A New Year and New Relationships! 21
    Luke 10 Hits Home..............................25
    A Revelation and A Challenge..................33
    Father, dear Father 37
    The Other Woman...............................39
    Torn Between Two Parents.....................41
    A Deception 45
    Solomon's Child 49
    The Birthfather..................................51
    At Death's Door 55
    Changes...59

Section II — Sought and Found
      Restorer of Broken Branches

    Love Answers 65
    To Mom With Love..............................67
    The Beckoning Mountain 71
    Peace at Last.....................................75
    Agape Love Does Work 81
    Exodus 2 Revisited 85
    Finding My Minor Child 87

Section III — Heartcries of His People
             Time Will Come

  The Founding of Adoption Triangle Ministry 95
  Heartcries of His People 99

Section IV — Illegal, Immoral, and Fattening

  An Inalienable Right. 143
  David vs. Goliath. 145
  The Case of the Missing Open Records Section 147
  A Matter of Control 153
  Restoring Rights and Privileges 157
  What About Open Adoption? .165
  Beyond the Shadow of Secrecy. 169
  Ambiguities in the Law. 173
  A System Built on Deceit Will Crumble. 179
  If He Inquires (Poem) 185

Section V — The Adoption Movement
            and Project Awareness

  Brief Background of the Adoption Movement. 189
  Do Birthparents Really Care. . .Forever?. 193
  Finding the Needle in the Haystack. 195
  The Awareness Project (What you can do to help) 199

Section VI — His Banner Over Me Is Love
             The Supreme Sacrifice

  The Trinity and the Triangle. 203
  Parables of Reconciliation. 207
  Called to be a Deliverer. 211

Postscript - The Ultimate Reunion 215

Adoption Activist Groups. 219

PREFACE

In my previous book entitled I WOULD HAVE SEARCHED FOREVER, I had just begun to touch upon several analogies between my Christianity and my adoption experience. In this book I have attempted to bring the two together in an effort to come up with a workable solution to the present adoption dilemma.

I don't recall exactly when I began to notice the similarities between my Christian faith and the surrender of my child, but very briefly I will explain my arrival at both.

In 1954 at the age of 15, I became pregnant 'out of wedlock' and surrendered my child for adoption. At that time I was told I would start a new life and the child I had just relinquished would be forgotten. It was to be that simple. It was not long before I realized that I would never forget the child I had given birth to. How could I have believed that I would or could! This was a life; a very real part of me. I have lamented over pets I have lost or could not keep. I should have known that I would never forget my child.

Nevertheless the secret remained in my heart for 22 years and was shared only with God. His comfort, when I finally learned to accept it, was my lifeline during those intervening years of 'not knowing'. He gave His stamp of approval upon my search and He ultimately answered the longings of my heart.

In 1967, in order to join the new church I was attending, it was necessary for me to make a public affirmation of my belief in Jesus Christ. Shortly after becoming a member, I was asked to teach Sunday School. Having four small children, I felt a sense of duty and obligation to do so.

Then one Sunday evening three years later, I heard a speaker from a ministry called Campus Crusade for Christ. They spoke of a weekend retreat for lay people interested in growing spiritually. I had two motivations for going. The first was the chance to escape for a whole weekend; and the second was that it might help me become a better teacher. I had no other motivation - though God did.

It was during that 48 hour period twelve years ago that I committed my life to the Lord and began to understand the meaning of a personal relationship. For many years I had known *about* Him, but now I *knew* Him. What a difference He has made in my life.

I share the above simply to let you, the reader, know where I am at this point in my life; a committed Christian of twelve years and a birthparent six years out of the closet with a completed search behind me. It is from this foundation that I speak, write, and intertwine 'the Trinity and the triangle.'

Sandy Musser
March, 1982

INTRODUCTION

As I completed my first book, I WOULD HAVE SEARCHED FOREVER, I realized it was a story that would never end. Adoption never does. It's a lifelong paradox from all three perspectives.

WHAT KIND OF LOVE IS THIS deals primarily with post-reunion experiences, which can be as difficult as the reunion itself. Since it's such a new phenomena, ongoing research is needed in order to provide insight for those who will follow in our footsteps.

It is for that reason I share the various stages of my own search, reunion, and reconciliation. I've also shared a few others. Some are great, some are fair, and some may be considered bad, but all are successful.

Success is coming to the end of the search. That's when wholeness begins; that's where completeness lies. Whatever the subsequent relationship might be can only be determined by the individuals involved. What may be considered great for one person, may not even be good for another. Throughout life we choose the relationships we desire to have or not have. Certainly this is true of those in the triad.

It is my sincere hope that you will gain new insights into the many faceted feelings and emotions that become evident when an adoptee faces the reality of having two mothers; when a birthparent realizes she can only mourn those childhood years because that precious time is lost forever; when adoptive parents recognize and accept the fact that though they were unable to contribute to their child's true heritage, they nevertheless understand the importance of that heritage to their child's identity.

The title has a dual meaning. What kind of love drives a person to search for someone they've never met? What kind of love causes an individual to expend time, energy, and money in pursuit of a stranger? What kind of love is willing to take the risk that fears may soon become realities?

The flip side of the question is asked of our legal system

that keeps adoptees' records locked up "forever". What kind of love is it that denies an adult the right to his cultural background, his heritage and his medical information?

It's asked of those adoptive parents who continue to lie to their adopted "children" and feel the need to go on playing the game of "let's pretend." What kind of love is it that keeps even the knowledge of the adoption a secret from those individuals?

It's a question asked of those birthparents who would remain in the closet at the expense of their adoptees' psychological or medical need to know.

And finally it's a question that is asked of the church - many of whom are presently working to keep the records closed and to keep the system status quo. It is fear that keeps records under seal. Fear is the opposite of love. Jesus spoke of a love that would dispel fear. Why is there fear surrounding the open records issue? Some of these fears will be explored in this book.

WHAT KIND OF LOVE IS THIS? What kind of "love" permitted slavery to thrive - what kind of "love" justified the Holocaust? What kind of "love" suppresses, represses, destroys trusts and guards the "secret"? What kind of "love" denies an individual the freedom of choice? That's the bottom line for the adoptee - the freedom of choice, which they do not now have. Should the system wield that kind of control upon lives by denying adults access to their own heritage, which by virtue of life itself is their birthright? When power controls, there is no choice! There is no choice for the adult adoptee in this country today.

As you make your way through this book, I would ask you to reflect on these questions. As you read some of the letters and accounts of triad members, ask yourself WHAT KIND OF LOVE IS THIS?

SECTION I

AUTOBIOGRAPHY

"The scarlet letter that once signified my condemnation has disintegrated and all that is left is a scarlet thread - a reminder of my redemption - my freedom from bondage. The truth has set me free."

Sandy Musser

What Kind of Love Is This?

There was a time long ago
  When I could only surrender,
Forced to play a painful role
  The role of a pretender.

Yet my love for you was stronger
  Than any man-made laws,
It was the driving force within me
  That kept me fighting for the cause.

And I would have searched forever
  Through any kind of storm,
Until the last piece was fitted
  And my "you" began to form.

I've been walking along this journey
  And have crossed so many roads,
I ran into many obstacles
  Trying to break the codes.

But now that I have found you
  and we are finally together,
I know without a doubt. . . .
  I WOULD HAVE SEARCHED FOREVER.

By Sherri Lynn

Reflections — April, 1982

As I hung up the telephone after talking to an adoptee who was just beginning his search, I began to reflect over the past six years. It had been that long since I first stepped into the world of adoption with all its ramifications, contradictions, and frustrations. The longer I was a part of it, the more baffled I became. As I gazed into space, the hundreds of conversations I had had with adoptees, birthparents, adoptive parents, social workers, clergy and legislators flooded my mind.

The WHY questions kept ringing over and over - "Why can't I know who I am, where I came from? Why can any clerk social worker, doctor, lawyer, indian chief look at my records when I can't? Why can't I get a copy of my child's original birth certificate? Why did the agency lie to me and give me misleading information? What is there about my birth and beginnings that I cannot know? Why should someone else tell me what's in my 'best interest' - I'm 43 years old!!"

The WHY questions asked by those in the triangle are asked as expressions of indignation; an indignation resulting from inhumane adoption practices that were supposedly done in the name of good. They are asked as expressions of righteous anger at a system that has violated the rights of individuals by setting up a process which denies those individuals a full awareness of self. It's a system that, presently constituted, affects the whole community and gives way to resentment.

I had to seek answers to these WHY questions and

discover WHAT KIND OF LOVE IS THIS? I was unable to rationalize the inequities from my Christian perspective and needed to test it in that light. I have searched the scriptures for answers. I will share some of them with you and ask only that you open your heart and mind to a new way of thinking about adoption and all it entails. There is no doubt in my mind that there is nothing in the Word that even alludes to the adoption process as it is handled in this country today.

The Rest of the Story

Hundreds of people have written asking about my post-reunion experience after reading I WOULD HAVE SEARCHED FOREVER. Most of them offered their condolences for the outcome of the book because my daughter had chosen to end our relationship only one short month after we had met.

However, I never viewed it as a sad ending; I was thankful to have had the opportunity to meet her. I finally had peace knowing that she did, indeed, have a good home. I could put all the unknowns to rest because now I had the answers.

The "rejection" was seen as one more learning experience along life's pathway - a chance for more growth. I see all of life in that light and know that change is always around the corner. No person or situation ever remains the same. We are constantly growing, therefore I always had hope.

WHAT KIND OF LOVE IS THIS continues where I WOULD HAVE SEARCHED FOREVER left off. July, 1978. I had just sent my daughter a card for her 24th birthday. Her last contact with me had been an angry phone call concerning a newspaper article written about our reunion.

Christmas, 1978. Having heard no word from her all year, I decided to write her a letter. With trepidation I jotted the following:

Dear Cindy:

    I have wanted to apologize for rushing our relationship. In retrospect I realize that I came on too strong and want you to know that I am sorry. My intentions of desiring only a friendship were real, though my actions seemed to contradict that.

    I thought you might be interested in knowing that I'll be a grandmother soon. Sherri is due in Feb., Linda in June, and my daughter-in-law (also an adoptee) is due in April. It's hard to believe, but we're all very excited about it.

    Had I told you that your son was born on my father's birthday? Kind of a strange coincidence, I thought. I guess he's starting to walk by now. That's such a cute age.

    I hope you and your whole family have a really great Christmas. It's such a happy time of the year and happiness is the thing I've always wished for you.

                    With much love,
                        Sandy

P.S. Please do not feel that you need to respond. Friends should never feel obligated and I mean that from the bottom of my heart.

    Around the middle of January I had made arrangements to have the book published. I wanted her to be the first to know and thought the information should come from me. In late January, '79 I sent her a copy of the book flyer along with a note that said:

I guess you didn't expect to be hearing from me this soon. I wanted you to know that my book will be on the market shortly.

I'm writing in an effort to convey how important it was for me to write my story. I needed to put it down on paper in order to release the many pent-up feelings and emotions I had from having to "surrender" you. We are told that once the paper is signed--that is the end. We now know that it's not the end --it's only the beginning--the beginning of pain, heartache, and wonderment. Now that you are a mother and have a child of your own, I'm sure you know what I mean. I'm also certain there is enough compassion within you for you to understand what I am saying.

I felt really bad that during our three meetings together we were never alone, making it impossible for us to discuss some of our deep feelings. I would still like to do that, at some point, so we might better understand one another.

Cindy, in closing, I want you to know that I would like you to have a share in any profits from the book. I didn't write it for the glory or for the money, but simply because I felt I had a story that needed to be told--the story of the hurt one suffers when having to part with one's own child; the need to dispel the fact that one can "forget" when one never does. It is a story that hopefully will help to change adoption procedures toward making them more humane for all parties concerned.

It is my hope and desire that you will

accept my sincere offer as a gesture of goodwill.

> Much love,
> Sandy

As I dropped the letter into the mailbox, I sent a prayer heavenward that I was doing the right thing. I did not want to offend her in any way or make her more angry than she already was. Her response came about a month later:

Dear Sandy:

I really don't know what I want to say. Your offer of a share in the royalties from your book is very thoughtful and generous.

However, I can't help feeling that you are trying to make up for the past. You really don't owe me anything! My feelings have not really changed since we last talked. I realize that you must be very sincere, otherwise you would not have needed to explain your actions and feelings to me.

I can understand how you must have wondered where your "baby" ended up. And I can appreciate all the years of wanting to know and not being able to. I hope this will ease your mind a little bit. Take care of yourself.

> Cindy

I was so happy to finally have some word from her since it had been well over a year. In March I answered her letter, but another shock was just around the bend:

Dear Cindy:

Thanks for your note. I appreciate you taking the time to share your feelings with me I hope you won't mind a comment in regard to me trying to make up for the past. I know that can't be done. I am convinced, as I'm sure you are, that you had a better life than I could have given. No, it's not the past, but the present and the future I think about.

The thing I know is hard for you to accept, understand, and grasp is that, in spite of the fact that I did not raise you, my love for you is real. You were a part of me for nine months and share my flesh and blood--that makes you important to me. I realize and understand that this feeling may not be reciprocated. However, that's o.k. because I believe that a mother's love is always stronger for her child than vice versa. I can't deny my feelings. That's just the way it is.

You can reject me, ignore me, or hate me--I will still continue to love you as one of my own. I have never negated the feelings of your adoptive parents and have always recognized them as your parents. But that doesn't mean I can't love you and be a friend to my now grown daughter.

Forgive my rambling. This whole adoption issue is so heavy! I often become angry at the system that imposed all this secrecy to "protect" those of us who never wanted protection from our own children or even asked for it.

In closing--an Easter thought: God sacrificed his Son for the sake of others. It wasn't an easy decision, but He knew it had to be done. There was no other way. I can relate to that. Through the sacrifice He made, my life has been fuller, richer, and better. That's what I wanted for you--a fuller, richer and better life because of my sacrifice.

At 40 I find that I am happier than I've ever been. Finding you has made a difference in my life. I thank God that He has allowed me to know you--if only for a brief time.

> With love always,
> Sandy

And then, a few months later, the bombshell dropped. In May, 1979, someone sent me a newsletter from an adoptive parents' group where my daughter and her adoptive mother had spoken the previous month. Her anger and indifference were expressed all too well as the words jumped from the page and seared their pain into my heart:

> "Cindy said she was always mildly interested in her background, but not in meeting her birthmother--she just wanted more information. She feels her mother is more interested in birthparents' rights than in her. She also felt her mother abandoned her. Cindy resents the fact she could be found."

It went on to make some untrue remarks about our reunion. To say I was hurt was an understatement! After some time had passed, I rebutted with the following:

Dear Cindy:

I thought I would wait awhile before responding to your comments in the adoptive parent newsletter. Now that time has lapsed, I've had time to digest it and have come up with two possibilities. The first one being that you could have been misquoted as I have been on various occasions.

The second one being that it is your intention to hurt me by distorting the truth. If that was your intent, then it may make you happy to know that you have succeeded. I am not made of stone--if I were, I would have forgotten about you 25 years ago and not sought you out, but I do have a heart--I do care.

My interest in birthparents' rights is because I ache for every birthparent. Do I care about their rights more than I care about you--NO! But I've been denied a relationship with you (for reasons still unknown to me). Therefore I'm putting my energies into a deserving cause - the right of every birthparent to know that their child made it to adulthood, the assurance that their child was not shifted from home to home as is so often the case, and finally the chance to be able to extend their hand in friendship to those who want it.

I don't know why you feel so antagonistic toward me. I really don't know what I've done to deserve it. But with a love that is and has been constant, I remain,

Your birthmother and friend

This particular letter brought an immediate response. She called as soon as she received it. She said she had kept every card and letter I had ever sent (that was encouraging news!), but that this one made her so angry that she ripped it up. She stated that she had not seen the newsletter and apparently they had taken what she said out of context. We then talked about trying to be honest and upfront with one another about our feelings, etc. The conversation ended on reasonably pleasant terms.

I then wrote the editor of the newsletter to correct some of the untruths and discrepancies:

> Dear Mrs. Nage:
>
> I feel the need to clarify a few things regarding the article about my daughter and our reunion.
>
> First of all, I never contacted Cindy's mother initially. I had contacted the minister who was the intermediary who, in turn, was to contact my daughter. Instead he spoke to the adoptive parents and was told that they did not feel it was the right time for us to meet.
>
> In the meantime I was able to obtain Cindy's name and proceeded on my own to write her a letter. Because of her age (22), I felt it should be her decision.
>
> Her mother then wrote me, and I responded to her; an exchange that was very caring in nature. My daughter finally contacted me by phone. We communicated that way over a two month period. Early in July I wrote and told her that I would be down to visit on her "special day"--her birthday. When I did not hear anything to the contrary, I went ahead.
>
> That hardly seems like a "surprise" visit as indicated in your newsletter. Our reunion was warm. We met for lunch once and on another occasion, she and her husband came to my home for dinner. It was at that time

she expressed a desire to "cool" our relationship.

For some reason I feel as though I've been cast in the role of a villain, when all I wanted was to meet my daughter and establish a friendly relationship with her.

The closed system of adoption affects all of us in the triangle. Along with you, I am working to open the lines of communication between the three parties. Since I've been denied that with my daughter, I guess it's being interpreted that I'm more interested in birthparent rights than in her--which certainly is not the case. However, I've been denied a relationship with her, for whatever reasons, and therefore have channeled my energies into birthparent needs.

Thanks for being a sounding board. I needed it.

Most sincerely,
Sandy Musser

Mid-July I received a call from Cindy inquiring about the book. I informed her that it was due to be published in a few weeks. She asked if I would send her a copy of it and I told her I'd be happy to do so, though I hadn't planned to. We chatted briefly, but the conversation was comfortable.

A few weeks later I autographed the first copy of I WOULD HAVE SEARCHED FOREVER to my daughter. In it I wrote:

THIS IS MY TESTAMENT OF LOVE TO YOU!

Again time passed. I had hoped to hear what she thought about the book and my perspective of things, but I heard nothing.

In September I was contacted by a Christian television station, inviting me to share my experience as a birthparent. Again, I felt it important for my daughter to know and preferred telling her myself, rather than have someone else tell her--after the fact.

I picked up the telephone, and felt good about doing so, but another shock! Her phone had been disconnected, and there was no forwarding number! I couldn't believe it. I had just spoken to her a few months before. My mind began to swirl--"What's going on? What is she trying to do? Why would she move without telling me?"

And so I began my search again, but this time with more ease. I contacted her mother-in-law, who informed me that they had moved back to the area and bought a home. Through information I was able to get her new number and address as well.

In late October, with pen in hand, I wrote:

Dearest Cindy:

> I am finding our post-reunion as much of a struggle as all that has gone before. I ask myself--"What is it you want or expect from this relationship?" and I'm not even sure I know the answer. Sometimes I think--"Gee, if we could just get to the point where we could pick up the telephone from time to time and say 'hi'--how's your life going?"
>
> I thought there was a beginning like that last July when you called and asked me to send you my book. I was comfortable and felt good about our conversation. Then I tried to call you to let you know about a national talk show I would be doing, only to learn you had moved. Not wanting to ever lose you again, I searched, but this time briefly.

Please forgive me if I annoy you--forgive me if you want me to disappear, and I don't. Sometimes I wish you would say, "Sandy, I really have no desire to have contact with you" (if that's what you really feel).

I love you unconditionally and always will.

Sandy

That was in late October of 1979. Two months later, I received my first card from her. It was a lovely handmade Christmas card and is among my cherished belongings. I was overjoyed. There was still hope! In early January I sent her a chatty letter about my kids, my job and my recent divorce. I had intentionally kept it on a surface level as again I did not want to offend or threaten what little bit of communication we had going at that time.

A New Year and New Relationships!

Winter flew by. Early in May, 1980, I attended the second annual national adoption conference held in Anaheim, California. It was representative of the 200 grass-root groups in the country joined in pursuit of open records.

During that week I had an opportunity to reconcile some deep feelings with my ex-husband. He had moved to California following our divorce and was not far from Anaheim. We met together and were able to share in a way we had not been able to do during our 20 year marriage! Why?

Did coming out the closet and dealing with the "secret" enable me to relate differently? Was my new self-esteem in operation? Was he more comfortable with the person I had become since finding my daughter? Was I more self-assured, more confident than I had been during our marriage?

We now share a unique friendship. We are reconciled, but not together. Reconciliation simply means to restore to friendship or a lack of enmity. We are reconciled in that way. Neither of us hold any grudges, bitterness, or anger for one another. We have each accepted our share of the responsibility for the failure of our marriage. We have both grown.

I have since come to believe that the marriage might have been saved if I could have dealt with the "secret" much earlier. Being forced to stay in the closet made me feel less of a person - that I was not worthwhile. I became a jealous, possessive person, fearful of losing another person I loved - just as I had lost my daughter. It was a great feeling to be able to discuss these things openly and to share them with the man I had spent half my life with.

That fall I was invited to speak to an adoptive parents' group in San Antonio, Texas, sponsored by Lutheran Social Services and the Council on Adoptable Children. They hold an annual "reunion" banquet for parents who have adopted through their agency. I was honored by the invitation and considered it a rare opportunity. The sharing that was exchanged was uplifting for everyone. It became one of the highlights of my speaking engagements.

I marveled at their acceptance of me. They didn't appear threatened by my presence, nor were they hostile. Certainly they were different. As I began to talk with the director of the agency, I discovered why. I learned that they are operating from a totally different perspective than most "traditional" agencies. More and more openness is being emphasized. Regular meetings of birthparents and perspective adoptive parents are held; an exchange of letters between birthparents and adoptive parents is encouraged. They are in the business of tearing down walls and building bridges.

An adoptive mother approached me after the meeting to express the love she feels for her son's birthmother since communicating with her by letter. She had reached the point of wanting to meet her and invite her into her home. That's what agape love is about! When we communicate with one another, we soon realize that we're not really adversaries at all, though the courts and most agencies prefer to see us as such.

Two weeks following the meeting in San Antonio, I was asked to lead a panel of birthparents at the Southeastern Regional Conference in Atlanta, Georgia. The topic to be discussed was "The Birthparent Dilemma". In my closing statements that day I mentioned that although Cindy and I had not had a relationship for the past three years, I still believed that someday we would. I never lost faith that the day would come when my daughter and I would be "reunited". I never dreamed it would be four days later!

On October 8, 1980 at 9:32 p.m. Cindy called. Would I come to dinner Saturday evening? WOULD I? Without her coming right out and saying so, it was obvious that she wanted a reconciliation. Later she told me that she was at the lowest point in her life - and reached out to me. She couldn't have paid me a greater compliment.

I had always kept the door open. During that three year period, I sent her a birthday card, a Christmas card and an occasional letter. She has since told me that my keeping in touch made it easier for her to reconnect when she was ready.

The following week I called to ask if she would be interested in attending a conference in Virginia Beach. Fortunately for me, it turned out to be one of her favorite resort spots. Only three weeks after her initial call, we were attending the Mid-Atlantic Regional Conference and sharing ourselves with those present. I can truly tell you that it was beyond my wildest dream. We had so much time to share our feelings openly and honestly. It was the beginning of our new relationship - a relationship that has continued and is blossoming to this day.

The message of the Prodigal Son parable is not only of the returning son, but also of the Father's open arms - waiting to welcome his child back. I waited with open arms and I believed.

In February of 1981, Cindy, her adoptive mother, and I had the pleasure of being guests on the Christian Broadcasting Network 700 Club Show. Our appearance together conveyed to those watching that agape love can bring about this kind of acceptance. It is agape love that unites us to one another.

The response to the show was overwhelming. Some of the letters received are shared in another section. It was on this show that the Adoption Triangle Ministry was introduced. The main goal of ATM is to bring the three parties of adoption together under the banner of God's love. The three of us were there to show the reality of that goal.

In August, Cindy and I, along with Mary Jo Rillera, taped the nationally broadcast Hour Magazine program in California. Mary Jo, founder of the Triadoption Library in Westminster, California, has recently written The Adoption Searchbook, a most comprehensive searchbook in the field. (See appendix for address).

We're all very grateful for the opportunities we've had to share our experiences and in some small way reach out and touch the lives of many.

Luke 10 Hits Home

Kansas City, Missouri, (the show-me state) was the home of the American Adoption Congress' National Conference in May, 1981. I looked forward, as always, to seeing old friends and meeting new ones.

Penny Partridge and I arrived Thursday evening. Penny, founder of the Adoption Forum of Philadelphia, had welcomed me into the movement five years before.

The first evening, an informal gathering was held. At one point during the night my eyes were drawn to a woman who looked somewhat familiar. Possibly I had seen her at last year's conference. As I watched her, I noticed that people seemed to shy away from her and tried to avoid her. Someone spoke to me, and my attention was diverted.

The following day was filled with activities and workshops. Again, I was drawn to this woman who looked years older than she actually was. Again, I noticed that people were avoiding her and would quickly move away as they saw her approaching. I watched for awhile and it seemed apparent that no one could hold a conversation with her. Once again my attention was drawn away.

Saturday was a pack-filled day. The general session in the afternoon was led by a speaker whom I had heard on several occasions, so I decided to return to my room and prepare my own talk, which I would give on Sunday morning. As I was passing through the lobby on the way to my room—there she was! She was sitting alone, talking to herself a mile a minute. Her hands were moving rapidly.

My immediate thought was of my youngest daughter, Sherri, and my second thought was of Jesus.

Six months earlier I had gone through the most devestating and trying experience of my entire life--the breakdown of my 19 year old daughter. She is now well. Her breakdown, which came on suddenly, lasted only a few weeks. But I recall that, at the time, my faith had plunged to its lowest depths. I questioned my loving God. How loving could He be to allow this? I told Him in no uncertain terms that I could see no good ever coming from this experience, and I questioned His wisdom of permitting this heartbreaking ordeal to happen.

There were fleeting moments when a scripture would pop into my mind *"When you pass through the waters, I will be with you; and through the rivers, they will not overtake you—when you walk through the fire, you shall not be burned; neither shall the flame light upon you* (Isaiah 43:2). Or I would recall the story of Job. Though he was tested beyond understanding, God had kept a hedge around him.

Aside from those brief recollections, my faith, for the most part, was at its weakest. I was ready to give up. I like Peter, was about to deny my faith and my God. I cried the usual,"How can you do this to me when I have been so faithful?" I could not pray. My dear mother called from Florida to tell me she was praying. I told her it was good someone was, because I was unable to. She said, "But, Sandra, my prayers are not for Sherri. She will come through. My prayers are for you—that you won't lose your faith".

I cry now as I write this and marvel at my mother's insight! She knew instinctively that *I* was the one in need of prayer.

Why am I sharing this very personal part of my life with you? This is why. Because when I saw Elma that day in May--I saw my Sherri--I saw my daughter and I knew that I couldn't look the other way.

My second thought, as I mentioned, was of Jesus--what would He do in this situation? Would He walk on by? I was going to give a devotional on Sunday morning. Could I walk on by?

I knew I had no choice but to go to her. I didn't even stop to contemplate it. It was as though I were drawn to her side. As I sat down beside her, I put my arm around her and looked directly into her eyes. I said "Elma, what's wrong?"

Elma began jibbering so fast that I couldn't understand anything she was saying. I abruptly said, "Elma, now hold it! Slow down! I can't understand what you're saying and I want to. It's important for me to hear what you're trying to tell me. Now go slow--o.k.?"

She did, and as I listened, I heard the heartache of a woman who had been abused in so many ways. She told me that she was a birthmother and had hoped to meet people here at the conference who would understand. She then talked about her bad marriage, how her husband takes her places, drops her off, and actually abandons her with no money to get back home. This was her situation now. Here she was in Kansas City, with no money to get back home. When he put her on the plane, he told her there was money in her suitcase for the return trip. There was none. It was quite obvious he was trying to dump her.

By now she was crying and sobbing. She went on to tell about a terrible crime that had been committed against her. It seems she had been brutally raped while working for the post office. She then made a statement that really grabbed me. She said "I came here thinking I would find friends that understand--people like myself who have been through a similar experience. But instead I'm treated like someone with a disease. I AM HUMAN, I DO HAVE FEELINGS." Those words still ring over in my mind.

After rambling on for awhile, I said, "Elma, I want to teach you a secret about communication. Communication is a lot like playing ball. I throw the ball to you and you toss it back to me. Now if you hold the ball, we can't play--the only way to play ball is by throwing it back and forth to one another. Communication is like that."

While listening to her talk, I became aware that the area of communication was one of her problems in relating with people. No one had ever taken the time to really hear what she was saying because they thought she was crazy. Then when she finally found a listening ear, she would talk as quickly as she could in order to be heard. It was a vicious cycle. I explained that she, too, had to be willing to listen to others and not monopolize the conversation.

She then looked at me thoughtfully and suddenly said, "How are your grandchildren?" Wow! I didn't realize she even knew that I had grandchildren. I considered that a real breakthrough. I said, "They are fine! Thank you for asking--would you like to see a picture of them?" (I was so sure *I'd* never be one of those bragging grandmothers!)

We chatted awhile longer and then I had to go, but I promised to try to help her learn the communication game. She thanked me and we parted.

There was a banquet that evening. I was already seated when I saw her come in and sit down. I immediately went over to her, told her how lovely she looked (she did) and reminded her of our conversation about communication. She assured me that she understood. As I observed her during dinner, I knew she had grasped the essence of "playing ball". She carried on a pleasant conversation with a birth-grandmother who was seated to her left.

Elma only needed someone to take the time to care and to listen. I happened to be at the right place at the right time and became the channel that God used--but it could have been anyone.

It was not until I arrived back in New Jersey and layed my head on the pillow Sunday evening that God revealed the purpose of the suffering I had endured through my daughter's breakdown. Had it not been for my experience with my daughter, Sherri, I also would have avoided Elma.

Fear would have kept me in its straits. Now I was seeing and operating through a different set of eyes. Now I could reach out to confused and bewildered people. Before I could not. It was then that another scripture verse became clear--*"When others are troubled, needing our sympathy and encouragement, we can pass on to them this same help and comfort God has given us"* (II Cor. 1:14).

Elma jotted me a quick personal note before she left. It briefly expressed her birthparent experience:

> "Sandy--it is difficult for me to talk about my 18 year old son and only child. It shouldn't have been. I was really able to raise him at the time, but coercion and brainwashing, power, lawyers, etc. have a lot of influence. Their system is not always easy to beat. And I've talked to my sister (who asked me to leave) and others, but the response is quick - 'Don't mention it to me again.' I feel like the lone wolf. I've had to battle for a living since I was 17--worked my way through college as a waitress, 30 hours or more a week with full-time classes as well. I have a B.S. in education. I've taught in Wisconsin and in Glendale, California. In Arizona I met the birthfather. He conveniently disappeared. So panic led me to my sister in the San Francisco Bay area--he was born October 27, 1963 at Chape Community Hospital."

Since the conference, we've been corresponding on a regular basis. Recently she sent me this poem written for her son's 18th birthday which was last October.

To Scott - My Birthson

I can't believe you're almost a man;
The little babe I didn't really plan;
I never held you in my arms or saw your face -
No, they took you right away,
As if I didn't even have a say.

But as I carried you I felt pure joy,
Because I never thought I'd lose you, my little boy.
I wanted you with all my heart and soul;
Yet someone else said it could not be,
Even though I felt you needed me.

The name I picked for you was "Shane"
From a western movie by that name,
And because a man of the western frontier
Had qualities that I've held very dear.

Truly he was a man of God;
His church was where pioneers had trod,
And though you're not now called "Shane"
I hope you'll live up to that name.

You'll never know the bitter tears
   I've cried through all these 18 years.
But you have another mother
And it's true you know no other -
May God bless her for taking you and giving
   you her love and home.

Eighteen is a giant step,
A milestone in your growing up.
So as you celebrate today,
I'll say a prayer and send your way;
But I hope for a moment, be it brief,
You pray for me and ask the Lord above
To remember us both with His great love.

That someday soon we both may meet,
Now it's my wish for you my sweet
That I'll see you even as you are -
And I hope that time won't be too long,
In the meantime "Scott" please be strong.

A Revelation and A Challenge

Saturday evening following the banquet I returned to my room. It was 11:30 p.m. and I still did not have my talk prepared for Sunday morning. Finally around midnight I pleaded with God to give me a message that would somehow touch those in attendance.

Almost immediately a conversation I had had with the conference chairman came ringing into my mind. He had called about a month before the conference to ask if I knew a minister who could give a devotional on Sunday morning. He was aware that I had recently formed the Adoption Triangle Ministry and possibly knew of someone who could fill that spot.

I apologized that I did not. Though we have a pastor on the board of ATM and other pastors have expressed an interest in our outreach, none of them would be attending the conference. I then volunteered to give the devotional. He thanked me kindly, but said that the committee preferred having someone with 'credentials'. It wasn't until that very moment that I realized what a thorn in my side credentials had been! I told him that I understood, and we hung up.

I was boiling within and furious to think that a piece of paper could disqualify me. I was angry and hurt. It occured to me that we seem to serve two gods in this country - one is money and the other is education. They go hand-in-hand. The more you "know", the more you make. It doesn't matter that you may be just as qualified - what matters is - do you have the piece of paper to prove it?

My initial anger subsided and I forgot about it until I received another call shortly before the conference. Apparently someone had been lined up, but was now unable to make it. Would I be willing to fill-in? I swallowed my pride and graciously accepted.

It was now late Saturday evening and all that had just been brought back to mind. The following message was given Sunday morning:

"You know - I never told Tom that I do have a Master's degree. Do you know how I got it and who presented it to me? I got it by attending the School of Life - otherwise known as the School of Hard Knocks, and it was the Master, Himself, who gave it to me. I'd like to tell you about some of the courses I had along the way that qualified me for this degree.

The first one I recall was a "Broken Home" course at age five. One of the subjects in that course was "How to Get Over Missing Your Daddy." It was a tough course because, you see, I was also separated from my brother and sister.

Then at age seven I took one entitled "Hating Your Stepfather for Taking the Love of Your Mother." I know this is a popular course today, but I don't think it's any easier now than it was back in 1946.

Now I want to stop here and emphasize that I'm not telling you these things because I want your sympathy. I don't. I'm telling you these things because each time I share them, I find I'm a little bit healthier; and also because I'm overcoming them and if I can overcome them, so can you.

The next course I had along the way was one of the most difficult of all and had a most profound effect upon my life. It was "Surrendering a Child to Adoption and Losing Your Sweetheart at the Same Time." Some of the subjects covered in that course were "You'll Forget" and "You'll Have Other Children." I failed "You'll Forget" - I never did! But I passed "You'll Have Other Children" with flying colors. I married at 19 and had four in four years! I quickly learned, however, that one does not replace another.

Several years later I struggled through the course "Raising Four Kids While Trying to Hold a Bad Marriage Together." I managed that for twenty years and recently completed "Divorcing Your Husband While Still Loving Him."

Twelve years ago I was fortunate to have had a "Spiritual Awakening" course. It was that particular course that gave me the stamina and perseverance to get through the others.

Six years ago I joined a course that has been most enjoyable. It's known as "My Adoption Family." That's you. I've now combined two of these courses - "A Spiritual Awakening" and "My Adoption Family" and formed the Adoption Triangle Ministry. It is through ATM that I have chosen to share the light I've been given concerning both spiritual and adoption concerns."

I then shared the goals and purposes of ATM which follow:

ATM was formed to unite believers within the movement; to take adoption issues and concerns to believers outside the movement; and to share God's love with all who cross our path.

ATM believes that everyone in the triangle has been affected by the closed record system. We believe that most adoption agencies were founded on religious principles (practically all private ones), and that ministers, lawyers, and doctors who were intermediaries in private adoptions *usually* did so with honorable intentions. However, due to societal changes and a better understanding of the bond that unites us, we now believe it is time for us to do the following:

1) be sensitive to all members of the triangle as well as to their family and friends, and be of service to those members in any way we can;

2) share God's love and endeavor to tear down the walls that separate us from one another;
3) speak out against the closed record system which we believe is unconstitutional and, therefore, goes against the very principles upon which our nation was founded; i.e. "We hold these truths to be self-evident, that all men are created equal and that they are endowed by their Creator with certain *inalienable* rights. . ."

The word "inalienable" means 'incapable of being transferred' and yet that's exactly what our legal system did back in the early '40's when the records went under seal. The adoptees' birthright was transferred. What our constitution said could not be done was done! Adoptees are being denied basic rights - liberty and the pursuit of happiness: the liberty to know their true nationality, their cultural heritage, the knowledge of siblings. Many suffer a lifetime when their 'happiness' could be attained by knowing who they are, where they came from, and finally connecting that missing link. As free Americans, certainly they deserve these basic rights.

Father, dear Father

The song "Father, Dear Father" has a special significance in my life. My parents were divorced when I was a child of five. During that period I had the privilege of staying with a great aunt and uncle on their large family farm in upstate Pennsylvania. Some of my fondest memories are of that old farm and those days. But so are some of my saddest.

How well I recall sitting at the old piano and playing that one song over and over--singing from the bottom of my young heart, "Father, dear Father, come home to me now, the clock in the steeple strikes one; you said you were coming straight home from your job as soon as your day's work was done. Come home, come home, Father, dear Father, come home!"

Why do I mention this in a book about adoption? Because I believe that separation by divorce is no different. I believe there is a drive behind the birth tie that is genuine. In many instances, the old adage that blood is thicker than water is true. That does not negate the love that one feels for someone else who has been the psychological parent. It simply means that there is a strong pull (possible chemical) or bond towards those who share our genes, to those we call birth relatives.

Daddy and Mom were divorced in 1944. I stayed with my mother and knew that she loved me immensely, but within me was a desire to know my father, to want to be with him, to spend time with him. I constantly sought out his love and acceptance until his death in 1975. As I stood by his casket that May day, with tears streaming down my face, I whispered "I always loved you, Daddy!" How I wish I could have heard those words from him.

These feelings are shared for whomever or whatever benefit they may be. I share them realizing that millions of children are experiencing these same kinds of feelings. I share them hoping that some father will recognize how important his role is and begin to relate in a more caring, sensitive, loving way. I share them because adoptees have expressed these same feelings toward a birthparent they've never known. And finally I share them knowing that possibly someone else will be able to touch home-base and thereby prevent the loss that I felt.

The above became an even greater reality in my life as I was going through my own divorce. My husband and I had been married for 20 years when our marriage finally came to an end. At the time of the actual separation and during the divorce, there was extreme bitterness and hurt on my part. Those feelings were unknowingly relayed to my daughters who in turn became indignant toward their father, loyal to me, and had chosen sides without me ever saying a word. My actions had conveyed what I expected of them!

When the realization of what was happening began to take hold, I knew I had to make it right. Admitting my responsibility for their attitude and actions toward their father was not easy. I had to acknowledge my own mistakes and explain that they should not feel the need to choose sides. I actually had to give my sanction for them to have a relationship with their own father! Only then did they feel free to do so. In doing this, I also found much of my own hurt and bitterness begin to melt away as I, too, forgave him and released the heartache.

The Other Woman

What causes these insecurities in our relationships? Maybe the following will shed some light.

There is a myth in adoption that an adoptee desiring to seek the birthparent is the symptom of a serious disturbance. Many adoptive parents feel they will never have to deal with this issue because "My child has no interest whatever—they've never even mentioned it". The truth is that an adoptee who desires to search is as well-adjusted and as stable as anyone else, but often will not discuss their desire to search in order to protect the feelings of the adoptive parents.

Adoption feelings and emotions within the triad can be similar to those felt in any love affair. In any male-female relationship, there is always the possibility of another person coming into the partner's life. But it is usually reasoned that if there has been a good relationship or if the love has been particularly special, the likelihood of that happening is less or nil.

How then does an adoptive parent deal with their own feelings of this crisis and pain when the realization hits home that the child whom they loved, cared for and cherished is now in search of another? How alike those feelings must be to those of a woman who has just discovered that the man she loves is showing interest in someone else. In the adoptive parent's mind, their child is showing disloyalty by even giving consideration to a search. They begin to ask themselves the same kind of questions a partner might ask - "What did I do wrong? Why is this happening? Didn't I give everything I could?" And then the accusations--"How long has this been going on? Why didn't you tell me before? How could we have been together all these years and I never suspected?"

Certainly the search causes self-introspection for all. It must also cause a painful suffering for the adoptive parent that only another adoptive parent can truly know. Suddenly there is "the other woman" to contend with. This intruder will surely cause a breech in a beautiful relationship. After all, it's a socially accepted fact that one cannot love two mothers! Everyone knows that!

They feel deceived - they loved and trusted. They never dreamed that this would happen - or did they? "Wasn't there some point in time - a certain question, a far-away-look that caused me to believe this day would come? What will people say? I thought I had been so open. I thought I had handled it well, but now with the reality of what's happening, I find that I am becoming a coward. I don't want to deal with 'the intruder' or the inference that her message brings. I don't want to acknowledge or admit that this 'other woman' gave my child life - a very precious gift. That reminds me of something I was unable to do. It reminds me of my infertility and I've never quite dealt with that issue. I didn't have to deal with it because this child brought joy that covered the pain and reality of my barren womb. The "secret" allowed me to pretend that we were just like a 'real' family - no different."

What is at the bottom of all this anxiety? Is it not competition - the feeling that now one is going to have to compete for the affections of the child? Is it not fear of losing the child to another?

Torn Between Two Parents

Like the song, Torn Between Two Lovers, many adoptees upon finding the birthparent have expressed torn feelings. There is always a strong sense of loyalty toward the adoptive parent, but also the strong tie of rootedness to the birthparent. If the adoptive parent has granted the adoptee permission to have a relationship with the birthparent, those torn feelings will be much less intense. We might call it 'freeing up' the adoptee to make their own choice; allowing them a relationship with the newfound birthparent without making them feel guilty for doing so.

When the adoptive parent reacts very hurt and obviously feels threatened, then the adoptee is bound by duty and obligation to suppress any feelings they might have for the birthparent. There is always the fear for the adoptee of losing the love of the adoptive parent or having them reject them. Unfortunately it is a fear that has been a reality for some adoptees.

Threatened feelings almost always stem from jealousy and jealousy from fear. What is jealousy anyway? Probably the nicest thing that can be said about it is that it's practicing a zealous vigilance over a possession or position. The possession in this case being the child and the position being that of parent. However, to be lovingly watchful isn't what we usually have in mind when we say someone is jealous.

The real issue then is that of guarding a possession or

position. This defending of possessions is common to all living things. When a bird flies into a fury in order to keep what it has, its intentions are clear. The jealousy is clearly stated; though its language is limited, its actions prove its point. Our human jealousy is not as clearly stated.

We have several ways that we express our jealousy since we have several kinds of language. These subtleties do not exist in the animal kingdom, and so confrontation is up front and straightforward.

When we're jealous, we may say we are supportive when our real intent is to undermine. We smile and offer sarcastic compliments in order to embarrass. We do one thing in public and the opposite behind the scenes. We even withdraw into silence and avoid others. We do all these things because of our jealousy.

The two obvious ingredients of jealousy are competition and threat. When we are offered competition on a threatening level, we usually panic into jealous retaliation. If we would just remember that we are diminished every single time we act jealous, then possibly such behavior could be avoided. The saddest part of all is that our jealous thrust is intended to put some controls on the other person, but almost always backfires on us. That's the reality of acting in jealous ways to guard our possessions or positions. On the other hand, sharing gives us just the opposite.

There are some techniques we can develop to manage jealousy. First, we need to recognize that jealous feelings are normal. Yet when we act poorly, we almost always degrade ourselves. We may not be able to control being jealous, but we can manage our reactions to it.

Second, we need to recognize the value of inclusive thinking. This will enable all of us in the triangle to share in what's happening to and for someone else. Jealousy is the result of thinking exclusively about ourselves.

Third, we need to recognize and appreciate the significance of the other person's needs and desires. We almost always tend to regard theirs as less important or meaningful as ours. Putting down another person or their efforts is the warning sign of jealousy.

Insecurity and fear are the culprits behind the trait and when self-esteem and self-confidence come into place, then jealousy will melt away. I can tell you from firsthand experience that the characteristic is destructive.

Yes, we in the triangle need to let go of jealous feelings. As William Penn so aptly stated, "The jealous are troublesome to others, but a torment to themselves." Work on ridding yourself of it!

A Deception

In June of 1981 I attended a CUB meeting in New Jersey before going to Florida for a few months. I had started that group four years before and felt quite a sadness about leaving. Interestingly, it was a meeting that wouldn't be easily forgotten.

We had several new people attend, and among them were a young attractive couple who represented themselves as a birthmother and her supportive husband. In less than a month's time, we were to learn that they were, in fact, an adoptive parent couple who had come to our birthparent meeting for the express purpose of soliciting information on searches. They had a hidden microphone and taped the entire meeting. As a result, NBC did a series on birthparent searches. There was a 'mystery man' involved known only as Jack. NBC termed their series "The Selling of Sealed Adoption Records".

I would like to tell you a little about Jack 'the mystery man' and then share a letter he wrote to birthmothers. . .everywhere. Jack is an adoptee, 50 years of age. The third of four children, he and his younger sister were removed from his mother's care and the home of his family after his father died. Jack remembers the day his mother's attempts to recover him resulted in her being physically removed from the foster home. When Jack was 12, he was adopted by his foster family but he never lost the need to see his mother again. It was a dream that fate cruelly denied him. His long, ultimately successful search yielded only the belated cold news of his mother's death.

His mission then became one of helping to spare others. To this end, he helped uncover information for many birthmothers about their lost children. It was a mission which resulted in his betrayal by his own peer group, by his termination of 15 years of employment with the State, by his now-tarnished record of public service and by a fine.

Here are his own heartfelt words that so deserve to be heard:

> Dear Birthmothers...everywhere,
>
> My quest in life has always been a secret desire to hold or touch my mother's hand, again. I remember so well the anguished look on my mother's face...her parting words that came forth that November day, spilling into the air to be lost forever, except in my heart. Her kneeling down, looking up at me, plays in my fantasy to this very day. It comes over me at unexpected moments in my life. It leaves and returns.
>
> I was just five years old, a most beautiful age to be held by a mother, when the sovereign State of New Jersey, in November 1937, allowed us a goodbye. I was then transferred to foster care and ultimately, adoption - a transfer that was to affect my entire journey through life.
>
> I never satisfied my quest to hold or touch my mother's hand. I arrived six years too late. She died with the thought that someday I would return. I can't begin to tell you how the grief still stains me.

To you, to each birthmother, to each birthparent, I want you to realize this: that part which grew within you and was surrendered will continue to grow into young children and adults eventually thirsting to know their heritage. Your child will never be fully replenished with all the comforts of life until they can reach out and "hold your hand". Do not wait too long, since time is so precious.

I vowed that others making up this adoption network would not suffer; that I, in some small way, would contribute in reuniting mother and child. Although during my sixteen years of enforcing criminal law, I upheld all principles required by the State, in my off-hours I was answering another law, the law of reunion. I knew no judicial body and legislative branch could legislate out of the hearts of birthparents or adoptees the right to search or look for their loved ones.

Recently my quest was interrupted. The NBC-TV story of Mystery Man Jack and the misunderstanding and preconceived fears of an adoptive couple all blended to delay your search and my quest for others. I don't know what will happen to me. This deepens the scars I already have. *It is ironic that the State that separated my mother from me has now prosecuted me because of it.*

However, the tremendous support coming forth, especially from birthparents I never met and the understanding of people outside the Triangle has propelled me. I now believe my demise is really not the end. The "Mystery Man" impact has created a nationwide resurgence, a renewal of faith, a binding together in spirit to begin reform for Adoption and create open records balanced fairly for all. You, the birthmother, the most powerful part in this Triangle must lead all of us since it was you who, out of love, did what you were led to believe was "best".

In closing, I say to you...please continue your beautiful journey forward, no matter the odds. Remember while I looked up at my Mother's face so long ago, you, too, looked upon your child's. Now, please go forth, so that some day you may "hold their hand".

What started out as a deception has become a reception. Society is finally becoming receptive to the need for adoption reform. We can never repay the Jacks of this world who have been willing to sacrifice themselves in order to spare others the pain they've known.

Solomon's Child

    The question immediately comes to mind - "Won't the birthmother "steal back" her child if she knows where that child is?" The 'wisdom of Solomon' is a story expressing the kind of love birthmothers have for their children and conveys the reason why they won't and don't--because they do not wish to see their children divided! Most have gone on to have other children and know what heartache it would cause in any family. This is not their intention or their purpose. They want only to "know" that their child is well. That in itself, brings a special peace.

    Let us recall the above-mentioned story taken from the Old Testament. King Solomon presided over a court of justice in Israel. Two women were brought before him and upon hearing their story, it was necessary for him to apply his wisdom to the case (I Kings 3:16-28). It seems that each had given birth to a son. They had been born three days apart. Like so many infants of such a tender age, they looked very much alike.

    One mother rushed excitedly before King Solomon and told him the following story. "It came to pass the third day after I delivered that this woman delivered also. This woman's child died in the night because she laid upon it, and she arose at midnight and took my son from beside me, while the handmaiden slept and laid it at her bosom, and then laid her dead child at my bosom."

We can practically hear the anxious voice of this mother speaking and we can easily visualize the expression that came across her face as she continued--"And when I rose in the morning to feed my child, behold it was dead; but when I considered it in the morning, behold it was not my son, which I did bear." Her instinct told her that the dead child was not her own. But now the other woman speaks up to tell her version–"No, the living is my son, she shouts, and the dead is yours."

King Solomon probably recalled that only a short time before he had asked God to give him an understanding heart and for wisdom to discern (I Kings 3:9). Now with this case of two mothers claiming the living baby, he surely needed it.

What fright came into the heart of the real mother. What boldness in the heart of the mother whose child was dead. A less wise person might have dismissed the case for lack of real evidence, but Solomon, in his wisdom, devised a clever trick. He commanded an attendant to bring him a sword and he held the sword in his hand. Surely there must have been fear and anxiety on the face of the real mother. Though she did not know what Solomon intended to do, she heard these fatal words from his lips: "Divide the living child in two, and give half to the one, and half to the other. (I Kings 3:25). The real mother hastened to say, "O my lord give her the living child, and in no wise slay it," but the other said "divide it."

May I suggest to you, dear reader, that many a birthmother has given up the fight right from the start rather than see her child divided in two. Can you begin to imagine the heartache of someone put in that kind of position and forced to make that decision. If so, then you can begin to understand the pain of surrender and all it entails.

The Birthfather

After I had completed I WOULD HAVE SEARCHED FOREVER, I realized that I had neglected to mention the birthfather to any extent--particularly after I had located my daughter.

To give a brief background--I had started dating him at age 13 and by my 15th birthday found that I was two months pregnant. I recall the feeling of wanting to be loved so desperately that I grabbed at what I thought was love--a physical relationship. I also realized that I was beginning to lose him and in hopes of holding on, I 'gave in'.

By our senior year of high school he was dating a mutual friend who he subsequently married. She was also the daughter of our minister - the same minister who "counseled" me during my pregnancy. As I reflect upon that now, it's ironic to me that *I* was the one in need of counseling since we were both members of his church. He was also the one who referred mother to another pastor who knew the adoptive family, and arranged the private adoption.

When I began my search, I contacted our former minister's wife about my desire to search for my daughter now that she was an adult. This minister's wife had been close to my mother as mother had been active in the church choir, and other church related activities. She became very angry and told me I would "pay" if I caused any problems between her daughter and son-in-law (the birthfather). Did I think I was doing the "christian" thing by digging up the past? She suggested I let sleeping dogs lie, that I had made my decision, that the child was no longer mine, etc. I informed her that I did believe I was doing the right thing since I had prayed about my decision to search and felt led to go ahead with it. She then told me that her daughter and son-in-law are very "respectable" members of the community and again some threats. I told her I was sorry she felt so adament about it, thanked her for her time and left. The Christian love spoken of so many years before in her husband's church seemed to allude me as I was escorted to the door.

I then wrote a letter to the birthfather expressing my interest in finding "our" daughter, told him of my involvement in the adoption movement and asked his cooperation should she be searching and locate him first. I stressed the fact that I did not want to create any problems for him or his family, but only wanted to find our daughter. I also requested some feedback from him concerning his feelings on the matter. The letter was sent by registered mail.

That was in January, and by April I had located her. He had not responded to my letter, so I did not know what his feelings were. In the meantime I had been in touch with a mutual classmate friend of ours who also happened to be an adoptee. Bill was also searching. Rather than write Len another letter telling him of my success, I asked Bill if he would be willing to get in touch with him and let him know. He agreed to do so and said he would express his own feelings of being an adoptee, so Len might better understand.

A few nights later I received a phone call from Len. When I heard his voice, I was taken back to my childhood and memories of our young love. It was then I realized that many of my feelings about him were yet unresolved. We spoke for 15 minutes or so. That special sense of humor that he possessed was still in operation. I felt 15 again. He said that his family (meaning his children) was not aware of the situation and naturally he wanted to protect them from this knowledge. I assured him that I had no intentions of disrupting his family, but that certainly Cindy had a right to basic information about his side of the family which I was unable to give. Therefore, the final decision would be hers whether or not to contact him concerning same. Again, I assured him that his family would not need to be involved in any way. We ended our conversation and I felt better just having the opportunity to talk with him about it.

Cindy has not expressed any desire or need to know any more than she already does about her father. By the same token, she knows that when and if she wants to, she will be able to get in touch with him and have any questions she might have answered.

Concerned United Birthparents has recently begun several studies concerning all aspects of birthparenthood. One of them involves the ongoing feeling of connectedness that many birthmothers feel to the birthfather years after surrender. As that research is completed, it will be made available to interested parties. Anyone interested in participating in the study may write to Gail Hanssen, Box 573, Milford, Massachusetts 01757.

In the meantime, it is a topic of discussion in the local rap groups around the country and the general concensus seems to be that most birthparents do continue to have unresolved feelings about the other parent.

At Death's Door

There are sudden moments when one senses life very deeply. We can be watching a news program, hear an announcement about a bomb explosion in a building nearby, see the mangled bodies and then suddenly a sharp awareness hits - suppose it had been ME. We are always close to death, but in the scurry of daily living this knowledge recedes into unawareness, numbness. However, I wonder if those of us in search of loved ones give more thought to it than the rest of the population. We are ever conscious of the fact that we are working against the hands of time, as evidenced by the following letters.

I've been corresponding, for the past four years, with a dear lady from Oregon who is 80 years old. Her first letter to me back in 1978 states in part:

> I was wondering if you could help me find my son. I was sent to an institution with my two brothers in Indiana and we were put out in separate homes to work. I got pregnant when I was 17 and I had to put my baby in the orphans home to board - not to have him adopted out! I paid $4.00 a week. He was born in 1918. I signed some papers before the judge which I thought was to prove that I was his mother and that I was working

in order to pay the board. When I went to the orphans home to visit him and take some gifts, they told me he had been adopted and would not tell me where he was.

I have grieved for him ever since. I'm sorry to burden you with my troubles, but I think of my son every day. I just had to tell someone to see if you can help me. I hope you understand how worried I've been all these years. I would be the happiest woman in the world if you could help me. I'm not well and want to see him before I die. I married his father a year after he was born and we had 12 other children. His father died in 1944.

Her most recent letter ended with the statement "I want to thank you for trying to find my son - I hope it won't be too late." Who, may I ask, are we protecting - her 62 year old son?? What is also so sad is the fact that this kind of thing is still going on today.

Another letter was from an 89 year-old adoptive mother who wrote and asked if we would search for her son's birthmother. He is now in his 50's. She said that his birthmother had requested a picture of him when she surrendered him for adoption and she had refused. She has lived with guilt ever since and does not want to die without telling her son's birthmother how sorry she is that she denied her that simple request.

Yes, we do struggle against the hands of time. We struggle to see our dreams fulfilled and to touch the face of a loved one. It is always our hope that our reunion will become a reality, but sometimes the clock of life strikes too soon and we find that death won out, as expressed in the following poem:

Thoughts
By Deby Raiford

How many times, throughout adolescence,
*   did I plan my trip to Albany?*
I'd demand my adoption record be opened.
This, I decided, would set me free.

Time flew by: days, weeks, years.
My plan remained, but an adult version now.
Twenty-eight years, where did they go?
Through marriage, divorce, marriage and birth of three,
I had matured, you know.

So I searched, and found,
My hopes were so high.
Just to touch your cheek,
To hear you answer my "Why?"

Murdered! Not just dead?
I can't understand!
Couldn't you have waited for me?
Didn't you see my outstretched hand?

The brothers and sisters are just not enough.
I needed you so. . . .
I feel cheated so much!

You were adopted too -
That makes us two of a kind.
We had the same problems,
I know what was in your mind.

I feel so much better,
Though still grieve in my loss.
My beautiful mother,
You're still in my thoughts.

Changes

The whole experience of the last five years has had a profound effect upon my life. The events forced me to examine myself and caused me to realize that the processes that were started in me no longer have any direct relationship to the pain of the past. I have a greater sense of my own worth. I am a survivor. I have survived! That in itself gives me a sense of pride and self-confidence. I know that I can live and work and love--in the midst of whatever life bestows upon me.

When I first began to come out of the closet and deal with my birthparenthood, much of my behavior at that time was one of mourning; mourning the fact that I would never know my daughter as a child. Those years are gone forever and can never be recaptured. I mourned illusions that had to be given up and parts of myself that I would have to release.

I've learned that adults can have a variety of relationships with each other and that one does not have to negate the other. I have since wondered if I am more philosophical because I am older. Could I have had these same feelings of acceptance at the age of 25?

I don't feel guilt anymore or blame myself for being young, ignorant, insecure. A strange new role has been created for me and I can say "You are the one who forced me to grow. I created you, but you in turn have created me".

In my last book, I shared a birthday poem I had written for my daughter. I am now sharing a birthday letter I wrote to myself on my 42nd birthday:

> "Congratulations. You're doing fine. You're more a woman and more yourself than you've ever been. I'm proud of how you've met life head-on hesitating only when fears deep within kept you from doing differently. But never from a conscious desire to hide. The things I like most about you now are:
>
>> You think things over more carefully.
>> You talk to yourself about decisions and give yourself time to study the feelings that eventually surface.
>> You have separated yourself from the demands of people you love at a profound level.
>> You care a lot and have a great sense of responsibility, but deep down you feel free of their wants.
>> Last, but not least, you can take care of yourself.
>> You are a nourisher of your own soul.
>> You've come to the realization that no one else can make you happy. Your happiness comes from within.
>
> I have no idea what will happen to you. I don't even know that it's necessary to think about it. Life has always been uncertain. There were never any promises or

guarantees. You just never understood that before. But now it seems likely that you can always find your way home--no matter what is going on.

I think the most remarkable change I sense is the way liking the person you now are has spread into all the crevices of your life and helps you relate to others in an empathetic way. Deep below the turmoil of life, you have found peace at an inner level. A warm glow glides through your being and a total acceptance of self. Congratulations!"

This poem expresses my general philosophy at this particular point in my life:

The Weaver

My life is but a weaving,
  between my God and me,
I do not choose the colors,
  He worketh steadily;
Ofttimes He weaveth sorrow,
  and I in foolish pride,
Forget He sees the upper
  and I the underside.

Not till the loom is silent,
  and shuttles cease to fly,
Will God unroll the canvas
  and explain the reason why;
The dark threads are as needful
  in the skilled Weaver's hand,
As the threads of gold and silver
  in the pattern He has planned.

SECTION II

SOUGHT AND FOUND

"In all of us there is a hunger, marrow deep, to know our heritage, to know who we are, and where we have come from. Without this enriching knowledge, there is a hollow yearning. No matter what our attainments in life, there is a vacuum, an emptiness, and a most disquieting loneliness."

Alex Haley

Restorer of Broken Branches

Lord —

You say in Your Word that "you shall seek me and find me when you search for me with all your heart."[1] I know that's true, because I did search for You with all my heart and I did find You. I only regret that I waited so long to begin my search for You.

And now, Lord, I am beginning to search with all my heart for a person out there somewhere who shares my flesh and blood. I'm not sure why I've waited so long to begin this search either, but maybe Your timing wasn't right until now.

I think about her a lot and I wonder if she's wondering. Is she searching for me? Has she thought about me over the years? Has she discussed me with You? Does she even care?

But, Lord, somehow I know and trust that You will lead me to her. The reason I believe that so strongly is because you've shown me in Your Word that reconciliation[2] is what You desire for all Your children.

Our roots were broken when we were separated, but they were never severed. And besides, You are the God of miracles who can restore broken branches.[3]

I will go on seeking with all my heart knowing You are right beside me, guiding me, leading me, and taking me to our grand reunion day.

A Seeker of Truth

[1] Jeremiah 29:13   [2] Matthew 5:24   [3] Romans 11:24

Love Answers

Webster has various definitions for love. Man has tried for centuries to define it. Multitudes of books and songs have been written about it. Certainly I am not about to reveal any earth-shattering discovery about what it is. How do you describe something you can't see or hold in your hand? If it's not tangible, is it real?

Man has divided love into three basic categories:

1. Eros - physical love, sometimes referred to as lust
2. Philo - the love one feels for a dear friend or parent
3. Agape - divine love - a love that emanates from God

I believe that only agape love can resolve the adoption conflicts and fears. It is this kind of love which tears down barriers and walls and builds bridges. Those bridges will allow us to cross over to one another into the land of compassion and understanding. Building bridges will allow us to embrace one another and begin to fulfill each other's needs--whatever those needs may be.

What kind of love IS this? How do you get it? Is there really such a thing as "unconditional" love - a love with no strings? Does such a love exist that isn't concerned with the fulfillment of our own needs?

The exciting and beautiful thing about "agape" love is finding out that you truly can love someone very deeply and yet allow him complete freedom to respond to you in whatever way God leads him to respond. This kind of love demands a kind of freedom that is impossible when we are bound by expectations.

We don't just love one or two people during our lives; we love many in varying degrees and in many ways. Love is not a zero-sum game in which the more we love one, the less we can love others. Rather, the more we learn how to love one, the more we are able to love others.

The answers should begin to unfold as we look at some triad members who have shown and experienced agape love. These personal stories emulate this special kind of love.

Two are adoptees; one in search and one who found "rejection". Three are birthmothers who found minor children; one has made contact, two have not. The other is a lovely reunion story.

To Mom With Love

A letter from a woman to her mother signed "with love" isn't unusual. It probably happens every day. What makes this letter a little unique is that I'm 28 years old and I've never written a letter to you before now. Even that isn't a first, I suppose, in cases where a mother and daughter are rarely or never apart. But we're different from those others. We've been apart a long time now, so wherever you are, Mom, this letter is to you with love from your daughter. It has been a long time, you wouldn't even know me if you saw me today. I've changed a lot. I'm sure you have, too. A lot has happened since we last saw each other. A lifetime of events have gone by. We're two entirely different people than we were then–twenty-some years ago.

That's a long time for a mother and a daughter to be parted. Even family feuds don't usually last that long. But our separation is different from a lot of other ones. Our lives split apart when I was too young to argue with you. I was only about a year old. Most children who lose their mothers do so only temporarily, in a crowded store or at a fair. I lost you forever when you gave me up for adoption.

I don't blame you. I may even have done the same thing if I was in your place. I don't feel bitterness towards you–only towards the laws that keep us apart. If you want to find me even half as much as I want to find you, then you agree with me that the laws that say we have no right to be together are wrong. Who has the right to make that decision for us--except us?

You carried me for nine months. You kept me for a year or more. You must have cared. These things, if nothing else, still make you my mother.

How can I send a letter with love to someone I don't even know? Maybe I do know you somewhat--through myself. When I sit crying at sad movies, maybe somewhere you're wiping away a secret tear too. When I do something clumsy, like bumping into furniture as I so often do, maybe you, too, rub a bruise and ruefully acknowledge your ungraceful way at times. When I look into a mirror and see my blond hair and blue eyes looking back at me, maybe sometime you looked into a mirror and saw a face not so very different from my own. When my love for animals comes out, who knows if you're not somewhere hugging your own pet? I get these things from somewhere, don't I?

How can I miss someone I don't even remember ever knowing? It's easy and it happens. Believe me when I say it does. When a see a beautiful sight, when I'm feeling sad, when I'm feeling happy, when special events come along--my wedding day, Christmas Eve turning into Christmas Day, my birthday--can you imagine how much I miss you then? How badly I wish you were around to share those times with me? Even on normal, ordinary days, I long for you to tell my thoughts and feelings to.

How do I tell you not to worry about me? That I'm ok. That my adoptive family is very good to me. That my husband is very special. That even though you may not be a grandmother in fact, you are a step-grandma. Maybe if I concentrate hard enough, you will hear me and know.

How can a supposedly grown woman search people's faces when they're walking down the street--and imagine that they're related to those faces? How can a heart almost stop beating every time the phone rings from hoping somehow to hear "this is your mother", or running to check the mail to see if by some miracle there might be news of you? It's easy enough, just ask me, I'll tell you.

Sometimes I fantasize that you're someone I know. A friend or relative, a former neighbor who's been kept a secret all these years. Foolish as it may seem, though, I like to believe that if I met you, I'd know you somehow by instinct or intuition.

Sometimes I scare myself by thinking you're dead. That there won't ever be any chance for us. That's a very frightening thought--at least while you're still in the world somewhere, there's still hope.

If I could meet you and give you anything in the world, I think I would give you my past, my memories. Then you might be able to see me as I really am rather than imagining how I turned out.

Even if I never do meet you, I'll still feel that I know a very important quality you have. I may not know anything about you in the way of looks, where you live, even your name, but I do know one thing. You're a very brave and unselfish woman. You gave me up so that I could have the kind of life you weren't able to give me yourself. I know it must have been hard. Who could ever give someone a more beautiful or totally unselfish gift? So, yes, I can say to you with love. Just as you may have said it to me when you said goodbye all those years ago. If you're out there listening, I love you, Mom.

> Your daughter,
>
> Cherie Weatherwax

Cherie wrote this letter in 1980. In 1982 she discovered her greatest fear had become reality - her mother had died in 1978. Those who have found the grave at the end of their search know the intense pain of that discovery - and the anger at the system that set up roadblocks to reunion.

The Beckoning Mountain

Would this feeling ever leave? It had been there for such a long time and I had almost grown accustomed to it. Yet, as I sat beneath the Christmas tree, I made a vow that before the new year was over, I would find my birthmother and at long last, the question mark in my life would be turned into a period and perhaps even an exclamation point.

In January I wrote a letter to the adoption home and told them that I wanted to know who I was or something about my birth kin. The search had started and just as surely as if embarking upon a journey, I knew without a doubt that I would reach that ultimate destination. I knew that the new year would surely bring about the end to so many questions that had remained unanswered.

In February a friend and I set out for Asheville, North Carolina for the talk that I had scheduled with one of the workers at the home. The drive was beautiful and yet it all seemed like an enchanted dream. As we pulled into the parking space at the home, I felt as though I were dreaming and I prayed that I would not wake up until I had all the answers. Little did I know that all the answers might never come.

Sitting across from Miss Murden, watching her read me certain facts from my family history was quite an experience! It was something that I wished on those who won't allow the records to be opened. Knowing that she had all the answers to the questions that I was asking and knowing that she held them all in her hand in that brown file drove me right up a tree. Yet, I tried to maintain a cool that inwardly I knew was at any moment going to explode. She was a kind woman and her manner of caring seemed truly real. Yet she could only tell me non-identifying facts. It was more than I had hoped for and with that information, I left for home.

Later that day I contacted a woman that was involved in helping people search. I gave her the facts that I had gotten and she told me that she would get back to me in a week or two. Exactly two weeks later, she called me and gave me my mother's name and the county in which she was born. She also gave me the name that my mother had given me--Phyllis Ann. . .All those years I had thought that my name was "Laura" and now I had discovered that it was Phyllis Ann.

March dawned brisk and cold, as did the contacts that I had during that time. I searched for leads and discovered that she had not been back home in 33 years and that no one knew where she was. I was able through the help of a very lovely lady to contact my cousins. All of them turned out to be very intelligent, caring people. . .very receptive and loving.

Finally I was able to discover an address on my mother. I wrote to her and within a few weeks, she responded. The dream was over and the reality of her years of hurt and rejection stung as never before. She wrote that I had upset her, that she wanted me to stay out of her life, that I was not to write nor try to contact her again.

For days, I seemed to move in a daze. I felt numb and yet throughout that time, I never regretted for a single moment what I had done. I prayed, I wrote and I worked my way through those days. Friends were a blessing and with their love and support, I still believed that it would all turn out all right.

Several weeks after that as I was walking to the mailbox, I felt strange. Something inside me seemed to tell of a letter that was waiting in the box. . .I looked at the postmark and I knew that once again, for whatever reason, she was reaching out. As I read her writing I knew that she still wanted to hear from me if only to answer the questions that she asked. She told me that she had two children that she loved very much. I knew that I never wanted to see her hurt and that if it meant never contacting her again. . .then that is what I would do. I wrote her back and told her that I loved her enough to leave her alone. I remember hearing one time that if you love something, you let it go and if it is yours, then it will come back to you and if it is not, then it won't. I began that day to adopt that philosphy for the feeling that I had towards a woman that for three months had cared and loved me. . .I felt only love and appreciation for her.

Not long after that I took a trip to Tennessee and met all my relatives. . .many cousins and a precious aunt and uncle. The love and fellowship that we shared was something that I would not exchange. Many memories were made that day and settled deep within me. The country was so magnificent and the people so loving and kind. What a special land . . .what a special time!

So now, I am back home, at work and busy being a wife and mother. My own adopted parents have been loving and supportive through all of this as have my family in Tennessee. There is a peace within me now that I never dreamed possible for no longer do I face a question mark but a period and yet it is as if there is no end to this story but instead a "to be continued".

Someone asked me the other day if I had it all to do again what would I do? It doesn't take love for me to answer that question for I know beyond a shadow of a doubt, that I would do it all over again. . .because for the pain of not knowing, there is now the comfort of knowing. . .and for the joy of knowing, there is a fulfillment and a love for many. . .

Yet, there are so many others, just like myself who

want to know, who should have the right to know and their search continues as do all of our lives. . .the right to know the question mark. . .the results of the search. . .the rejection or the acceptance all have to be dealt with. . .

No it has not been an easy thing to do, but it has been a beckoning mountain all my life. I feel as the mountain climber who finally after months of scaling the mountain can finally see over the top and from where I stand. . .

the view is worth it all!

Marsha

Peace at Last

In 1964 I surrendered a daughter to adoption. Emotionally, I have never been able to make that same surrender in my heart.

My first reactions to my pregnancy were of fear and shame. Because of my unwed status and younger children in my family, I knew I could not remain at home. I went to my doctor who advised me to talk to a Catholic Agency in the area. I made an appointment with the head of the agency, who happened to be a priest. My interview with him lasted about one hour. He did most of the talking as he knew I was extremely upset. He told me he planned to send me to a home for unwed mothers, where I would await the birth of my child. He encouraged the adoption of a child born out of wedlock as the best solution for mother and child. He offered no other alternatives nor did he make any other suggestions. A secretary then took pertinent information from me.

I had not told the birthfather of my pregnancy. My reasons at the time seemed important to me. He had just been discharged from the Army and just starting back to work. He was restless and I knew he needed more time to readjust to civilian life. In my heart, I felt my pregnancy would not be happy news to him. I felt that my pregnancy, before marriage, would hinder my relationship with my future in-laws. Emotionally, I knew I could not tolerate any type of confusion during this early stage of pregnancy. By not sharing my pregnancy with him or his family, I thought I would have the peace I needed at that time. He had telephoned me a few times after I terminated our relationship. I talked with him each time he called but I discouraged any visits from him.

Early in my fifth month of pregnancy the agency notified me that I was to enter the home the following week. Before going to the home I was to stop by the agency for last minute instructions. At that time they gave me a false name to use for the home and hospital and told me it was being done for my protection and privacy. The home was new and beautiful, away from the city, housing about forty girls at one time. The atmosphere was depressing. Most of the girls were emotionally upset and kept to themselves. I felt very much alone. While at the home, we were not questioned or pressured in any way. A nun from the agency would come once a week to talk with us privately and/or as a group. She told us if we were planning to surrender it would be best for our child if we surrendered as soon as possible. She also stated that if we should decide to get married in the future, there was no reason why we had to confess to our spouse about this child born out of wedlock. There was no need for anyone to know. When the time came for us to leave the home, we should forget the past and begin a new life for ourselves.

While at the home I often thought about the birthfather. A couple of months had passed in which I had not seen him. I wondered how he was, what he was doing with himself and if he had met anyone new. I wondered too, if he ever thought of me.

When time neared for my child to be born I was taken to a nearby hospital. When my daughter was born I was told I was allowed to see her and have her for feedings while in the hospital. I feel very fortunate that I was emotionally strong enough to see and feed her. Each time they brought her to me, I held her very close and kissed her many times. I knew she could not hear me, nor would she understand what I was saying, but I told her how much I would always love her. Those four precious days we were together are very special days in my life and I have reflected back on them many, many times. Two weeks later I surrendered her to adoption. The only information I was given at that time was that my birthdaughter was going to a Catholic home and I was never going to see her again.

As time went on the pain of separation from my child grew stronger. I missed my birthdaughter terribly and my heart ached to see and hold her once again. I went back to work–physically. Emotionally and mentally I had to force myself to function. I could not take my mind off my birthdaughter. Life had no meaning, no purpose for me. I lost interest in my friends and family. I found it hard to participate in family affairs. It became harder and harder to laugh, to be happy, and I did not want to be around happiness. I wanted to be alone. I felt empty and drained on the inside. My body was tired, my mind wide-awake. I could not eat. I had trouble sleeping. When I did fall asleep I was constantly dreaming--the same dream all the time. I would dream I surrendered my birthdaughter to adoption and I was suffering the aftermath of that decision, reliving in my sleep what I felt while awake. I would wake up crying, turn my light on and look for my birthdaughter's crib in my room. When I didn't see her crib, I realized that my dream was true. Often, before going to bed I would ask God to please take me quietly during the night. When I would awake in the morning, I would cry, because I was awake and alive, and I didn't know how I was going to make it through another day. The emptyness and heartache I felt would not go away. I worried constantly about my birthdaughter. Where she was, was she alive, was she well, what was she going to think of me for surrendering her, etc. . . . The first five years following surrender were almost unbearable for me--as I was struggling through ordinary everyday living. During this period I hardly ever thought about the birthfather. Since five years had past, I felt I had put him out of my heart forever.

After the first five years I did begin to adjust to life without my child. The depression was not as constant. There were days when I did not think of my birthdaughter--there were days when I could think--happy thoughts of her. I learned to take advantage of these times for I did not know how long this happy period was going to last for me. Whenever my spirits were high, my heart light, I tried to resume my life in a normal way.

For some unknown reason, I started to think more and more about the birthfather. I had feelings of guilt for not telling him of his child. I began to question myself as to why I did not tell him. I was sorry I had not. Perhaps, due to my emotional condition, I underestimated him. I often thought if I had shared it with him, my life and the decisions I had made, could have been different. I often wished the three of us were together.

To this very day I deeply regret surrendering as I have not yet completely recovered. I do not expect to ever be the same person I was before pregnancy and surrender; for as a result of that pregnancy and surrender, a part of me no longer exists. I truly thought the feelings I had developed for my birthdaughter would diminish in time, due to separation. I wanted her to have a mother and father in a secure and loving atmosphere. Knowing she would have this, I thought I would be satisfied. I had never been a mother before and I did not know my feelings for my child were natural, human, and here to stay forever. Little did I relize, this child I was surrendering, was to be my only child.

While I was pregnant I only thought of the present time. I never gave much thought to the future--like going back to work and maybe someday being able to care for a child myself. I never thought ahead--about my birthdaughter growing up, saying her first words, getting her first tooth, taking her first steps, going to school, etc. . . . As time passed and I visualized in my mind and heart these events taking

taking place in my birthdaughter's life; realizing I was not going to be there to share them with her, was heartbreaking.

For twelve years I never talked about my birthdaughter to anyone. In 1976 there were a series of articles in a local newspaper relating to adoption. I was fascinated by these articles. For the very first time I was reading about birthmothers and adoptees successfully searching and finding one another. I could hardly believe what I was reading. I had no idea that this was happening. When my agency told me I would never see my birthdaughter again, I truly believed them. The articles also stated that many adoptees were experiencing emotional problems in dealing with their adoption status. This upset me very much as I never meant to create any additional problems for my birthdaughter by surrendering her. The articles also mentioned different organizations that were forming for those involved in adoption. I joined as many as I could. I wrote to different people mentioned in the articles to enable me to learn more about adoption. I began to collect every newspaper/magazine article and book I could that related to adoption. As a result of this new knowledge I had obtained, on a very low-keyed basis, whenever I was emotionally able, I began to search for my birthdaughter. In 1979 my search was successful. I have no plans to contact my birthdaughter while she is in the minority years. I do not intend to interfere with her life or to upset her adoptive family in any way. I have seen her from a distance many times. She appears to be healthy and happy-- and for this I am truly grateful. I'm hoping and praying that someday she will have the need to know me and will take the necessary steps to find me. I have been in touch with my agency, updating information about myself and letting them know I will always be available to my birthdaughter. I feel confident that my birthdaughter's starting point will be the agency from which she was adopted.

By knowing my birthdaughter is alive and well, I am experiencing an inner-peace which I have not known in a long time. I am able to function better, life seems easier and I am able to give more of myself to others. According to information I have been able to obtain regarding my birthdaughter and her adoptive family, I feel her life should be happy. As far as the birthfather is concerned, I have decided not to inform him of his child at this time. If and when I should have a reunion with my birthdaughter, I will tell her about her birthfather not knowing of her existence. If she should desire to meet with him, some how, some way, I will do whatever has to be done at that time. In knowing who my birthdaughter is, where she is, etc. . . .does not erase the heartache and pain involved in surrender. It does make the burden lighter and easier to deal with. As a birthmother, I feel that my surrender could have been less painful, my life more normal, had I known the welfare of my birthdaughter during the years following surrender. It would have helped me accept and adjust to surrender, had I been able to return to my agency every two, three or five years for non-identifying information regarding the welfare of my birthdaughter and her adoptive family.

Although I realize now, I had made a decision during an emotional crisis in my life, a decision was made and I cannot go back and undo it. I must live with the consequences of that decision.

It is my personal wish, that in the near future our adoption laws will be revised to equally benefit and enable all three parties involved in adoption, to live a more peaceful and fulfilling life.

A Caring Birthmother

Agape Love Does Work

On December 20, 1979 at 3:00 p.m., I saw the daughter I had not seen since I surrendered her October 5, 1957. It was quite an unusual experience for all concerned.

We had exchanged letters and phone calls for about six weeks. I had put a few leading items in the letters that were passed through the agency. It was these "little bits" of information that let her trace me to my present locale. She then got my phone number from them after letting them know that she knew where I was. Two weeks before I met her, I spoke to her on the phone for the very first time.

I told her I could not give her up again so she should be sure of what she wanted before giving me her name and address. She had given it a lot of thought beforehand and had on occasion "chickened out" but had made up her mind to know me, her birthfather and two sisters and brother. (Her "full siblings" have since written her of their love for her and their long wait to find her. They had always known about her). We have shared many strange experiences over the years, much as separated identical twins experience.

Her adoptive parents have no other children. They were led to believe that I was dead, so nobody thought they would find me or any siblings. When they found out I was not dead, they wanted to find me and my family.

At the initial meeting with my birthdaughter (all

the aspects of surrender and adoption had been taken care of by letter and phone), one of the first things she wanted to know was her "nationality" and "why was she adopted". I told her why when she asked. I was alone with her for about ten minutes. I cried a little when I saw her and said "My baby is all grown up". She did not cry, but seemed stunned. We had exchanged pictures beforehand. She told me it seemed so strange to look at a stranger and say to yourself, "This is my Mother". About a week before we met, she told me on the phone, the song "Deje Vu" by Dionne Warwick was our song (hers & mine).

    Her adoptive parents met me ten minutes after our initial meeting. They were very nice and we took pictures. The adoptive mother looked scared and I tried to comfort her. I told her that I always believed God had chosen this route for me and my birthchild and I was sure he also chose her to raise "our" child. I told her also, I didn't understand it all but I'm sure what God does is right. The adoptive parents took me to their home and insisted that I stay with them. I had to refuse because I had already agreed to stay with my mother who lives about two miles away from them. The adoptive parents had just moved to that area a year before. She has lived in Georgia for the past four years. I felt that they should have time with her alone and she should have time to sort out all this emotional input. I was welcomed in the adoptive parents home and I had Christmas dinner there. I took them and my daughter to meet my mother that night. During the next few days, she met my brother and sister and younger cousins, some of my aunts and uncles on both sides of my family. All went exceptionally well. She was a "star" and loved every minute of it. She was in New Jersey for seven days and we went to meet her birthfather and his family during this time. That also went exceptionally well.

    She went back to Georgia and I joined her five days later. It was then I really got to know her. I spent six days with her. She was very proud of me and told anyone and everyone about me, who would listen, of what a strong and fine person I am. She told them of the "great love" that God gave to me to pass on to her. She had never experienced bitterness as many adoptees do, mostly because she was led to believe I was dead. She has totally accepted the whole thing but wishes I could have raised her so she could have known her siblings as they grew. Her adoptive parents are older than her natural grandparents, therefore I have more modern views. She also has to make up a lot of lost time with siblings.

She has an intense love for her adoptive parents and I insisted she take care of their wishes first, should there ever be a conflict. I had to explain to her that I wouldn't think much of her if she could forget all they had done for her all these years. It was not necessary for me to say all this to her, as she had it all figured out, but I wanted her to know where I stood.

When I left Georgia to come home, her adoptive parents went through a very bad emotional time adjusting to all that had happened. While I was in New Jersey they had control of the situation, but down in Goergia, they did not. At that time they let their fears get the best of them and I fully understood. I suggested to my daughter that she keep me very low-keyed for awhile until they feel better. The situation has eased considerably. I sent a thank you card and a picture of the three of them together that I had taken at our reunion.

I talk to my daughter about two times a week and when possible she will come to Montana to meet her stepfamily. I received a Valentine card from her that says "Mother, I'm so glad I happened to you! Happy Valentines' Day". She wrote under it "I really mean it". When she calls me up, she calls me Ma. She calls her adoptive mother Mom and her adoptive father Daddy. For a long time she didn't know what to call me so we used song titles. She called me "Deje Vu" and I called her "Little Green" (a song about an adopted child). Also her favorite color is green. We are very truthful with each other, even if it's not a pleasant subject. She wondered why God wanted us to meet. My answer was "you have been given everything a child could want and you have been spared a lot of pain that your siblings had. The only thing *I* can offer is "roots, my faith and my God". She is in the process of accepting all.

There was only one tense moment in the entire reunion with her siblings. One day after meeting them, she became a little irate about not being able to grow up with them. We had to go all over the events leading to her surrender. She could not understand at that time and became a little emotional about it. The only answer possible was to compare her to Moses. For some reasons known only to God, for her to become who she must be, she had to be raised by her adoptive parents.

She celebrated her 23rd birthday with us. We invited a lot of people and had an old west type of celebration. We did a little touring of the area, but most of her time was spent with her siblings. Her youngest sister is eight years younger and they didn't have a lot in common, as she does with the other two.

On August 2nd my son flew to Georgia. Her parents were very happy about her brother being there and have invited him to come to their house with her at Christmas.

Agape love really works!!

                                                         Pat

Exodus 2 Revisited

Dear Rabbi,

I am a birthmother with a twelve year old son that I surrendered for adoption when I was sixteen. I found out that my son, who lives only about four miles from me, was adopted by old friends of our family.

This summer we all went to the same pool. My children from my marriage became good friends with the son I relinquished and his adoptive brother. Next year he and my ten year old daughter will attend the same intermediate school in our township. They are such good friends now, who knows what could happen in high school? What about dating, marriage? Jewish law forbids incest, and it is a real problem among adoptees. One couple found out shortly before they were to be married that they were half siblings.

My situation is purely a coincidence. My son was placed for adoption with a reputable adoption agency, and all records were sealed according to law.

I have not told him or his adoptive parents who I am, for I don't see what can be gained at this tender, young age. At times I feel guilty for deceiving his adoptive parents, but I don't know if they would be able to handle it emotionally at this time, and I am afraid of their rejection. He knows that he is adopted, but his adoptive mother openly talks about her pregnancy and about the genetic reason for the color of his eyes. It is very disappointing to me that she is not more accepting of the fact of his adoption.

He is a bright, beautiful child, and we are very good friends. As such, he and his adoptive brother attend outings with my other children. Also, they have been spending time with us on the days when there is no school, as his adoptive mother works full time. It is a paid babysitting arrangement.

I have loved my son very deeply from the moment I knew that I was pregnant, and I would never try to hurt him or his family.

On page 280 of "To Be A Jew" Rabbi Hayim Halevy Donin says of adoption, "Jewish law regards the relationship between natural parents and their offspring to be irrevocable." I feel that adoptees are people with feelings. They have a right to know they are adopted, and the adoptive parents have the responsibility to tell them as early as possible.

It is my experience that most birthparents and adoptees want to know each other. Most adoptees feel that the magic age of eighteen, the age at which most legislators would like open records laws to apply, is a myth. Most adoptees have strong needs to know the mother that brought them into the world long before then. If the love and communication between the adoptive parents and adoptee is strong, then they need not fear the friendship of a birthparent. The understanding and acceptance of the adoptive parent can only make the bond strong.

This letter may read like a poorly written soap opera, but I assure you that it is true. His family and my family attend the same synagogue, we all live in New Jersey, and we may be members of your congregation.

Yours truly,

A Mother Who Cares

Finding My Minor Child

If God has taught me anything through my experience as a birthmother, and with adoption, in general, He has taught me patience. I have had real life experience in knowing what it means by "in the Lord's time."

I've always believed that things happened for a reason, even when things hurt me or I didn't understand. As I look back at this past year, and in particular the last sixteen years, I marvel at what the Lord has done in His timing–and in spite of me.

You see, I have a daughter who has just turned sixteen, and 16 months ago, we were reunited and have an ongoing relationship. I started searching for her when she was 14. I always thought that if she inherited my curiosity, she would come looking for me when she was 18. However, I was going to make it as easy as possible for her, and figuring it would take about four years to find her, I started shortly after her 14th birthday.

My closest family members and friends were supportive of my venture except for negative responses from a few relatives and friends. It was these negative responses that seemed to weigh most heavily upon my heart, so I turned to the Lord and prayer, asking Him to guide me and give me the assurance that this was the right thing to do. I received assurance and to this day truly believe that it was only by the

Lord's doing that Courtney and I have had a reunion and continue to develop a relationship. In less than three months I had the lead I needed to get the piece of paper with my daughter's adopted name on it.

"Courtney, Courtney." Over and over again, I said the name. I finally knew her name. I could call her by name when I prayed. Now, instead of praying "bless and protect my daughter," I could say "bless and protect Courtney, and let her know I love her."

I have never known such joy and excitement--the lighthearted and peaceful feeling I had at that moment. If God had appeared in the flesh and hugged me, I couldn't have loved Him more for the gift he had just given to me, and I knew it was just the beginning of many prayers yet to be answered.

I had been to the agency three times in the last two years updating files and requesting that they contact my daughter's parents to tell them I had been there and was available for any information if they wanted or needed it. Each time they tolerated me, but told me in no uncertain terms that it was against agency policy to let adoptive families know that the birthmother had updated the files or been there, unless the adoptive family were to ask.

Knowing the agency hadn't been helpful in the past and knowing they would be horrified to know that I now knew my daughter's name and address, I decided to use an adoptive mother to be my intermediary to Courtney's parents. Carol, my intermediary and I corresponded for many months before the letter was written and sent. Again, another of God's coincidences! When Carol and I first started corresponding, she lived far away, but was in the process of moving to a town much closer to me. She not only became an intermediary for me, but one of the most important people in my life. She loved me, nurtured me, and even took on my suffering, and she continues to act as my sounding board and counselor as I encounter "unknowns" in the relationship.

Six months after finding Courtney, the letter was written and mailed and received within eight days of Christmas. Courtney's parents experienced the anger and shock that any adoptive parent must feel when they are taken by surprise, but again God was definitely in charge of this relationship. Courtney had gotten into the letter and questioned her parents about its contents. Because they've always been honest with her and answered the many questions she had over the years, their love for their daughter gave them the courage to speak with honesty that night. They told her about me and said they would give her three days to think about whether she really wanted to know me before doing anything further. Each day they asked her if this was really what she wanted, and each day the answer was the same--yes!

On December 20th at 10:15 p.m. I was talking to my daughter's parents; the people who had raised her, watched her grow, given and received her hugs and kisses. The father told me about the first day she came into their lives right up to that very evening and I felt like I was watching a movie unfolding, as I mentally envisioned my baby grow into the 14½ year old she was then. When her mother got on the phone, she didn't say much, but she didn't have to. We seemed to understand where each other was coming from without too many words needing to be spoken. When I told her that this would be the first happy Christmas I've had in 14 years, she said she knew. And I knew at that moment that this woman had to be a very empathetic person, and probably a strong force in the decision being made that would allow me into their lives.

But the miracle didn't stop there. I thought the parents would talk to me, get the needed information, and that would be it--until Courtney was 18. But then her father said, "Well, we've talked enough. Courtney isn't going to be able to wait much longer. I'll put her on now. . ." And there she was on the phone. My first words were something like, "Hello, Courtney–I just want you to know before I say anything else that I've always loved you. There hasn't been a day go by that I haven't thought about you. . ." Then the tears, and lots of questions. We talked like two friends that had been separated for a long time and had a lot of catching up to do. . .but then, I guess we are, aren't we?

One of the first things Courtney said was "My parents were going to help me look for you the summer of my 18th birthday, but now we won't have to!" I never thought I'd be happy paying a phone bill, but that was the best one I will probably ever pay.

On January 23, history was being made around the world. The American hostages were returning home to America from Iran, being reunited with family and friends. In a little agency, in a little town, adoption history was being made, but not recorded - except in the hearts of my husband, Courtney's adoptive parents, Courtney and myself, as we came together once again; mother and daughter embracing, touching, crying. My arms that had ached to hold her were now fulfilled.

Peace, love, happiness, but mostly God was in that room. This time when I walked out of the agency, I was not alone.

This past year Courtney and I have gotten to know each other better through letters, phone calls, a couple days spent together, and two overnight stays at my home. Our relationship has been like the unfolding of a flower. Sometimes I'm fearful that the door will close and I hurry to tell her as much as I can. But the door hasn't closed. I pray for guidance all the time. I often feel as though I'm walking on egg shells because I'm trying to guess how her parents might feel about certain situations. I constantly roleplay trying to feel what they might be feeling, if the tables were reversed. I admire her parents. If I could have handpicked them, they would have been my choice.

I know God is a part of this whole relationship. Whenever I write or call or see them in person, I always pray that He be in our midst. I ask for His guidance because He does know their thoughts and He dictates my actions accordingly.

I know Courtney is what she is today because of the love, honesty, and goodness her parents had in raising her. Their honesty has given her security. Shortly after our reunion, I received a letter from her mother in which she said "I've noticed a loving change in her since all this happened. She will tell me at least twice a day she loves me, and will hug me, as much as to say she knows how I feel about everything and wants to assure me she loves me. She is very understanding about you, and I think it made her very happy that you found her." Her parents didn't lose her by my entry into her life; she feels the bonds to them stronger than ever.

As Courtney and I have corresponded, she drops pearls of wisdom that I marvel that one so young can be so wise. Shortly after our reunion, she wrote, "I'm very glad that you've come into my life. You've kept it from being a boring school year! I also like how you care about me." In another letter she said "I'm glad that you care about me. It feels nice when you wake up in the morning and know you've been found. I'm really glad that *you* found *me*. If *I* found *you*, I would have always wondered if you cared enough to look for *me*. I was going to start looking for you when I was eighteen, but now I don't have to search! Before you found me, I always asked questions. I pestered everyone, but nobody could tell me anything." (The agency had given very little of the information that I had given them to the family).

Courtney is very much a part of our family. My husband and two sons accepted her as part of us from the first phone call. She brings vitality, freshness, beauty and strength into our family. I feel like a whole person now. I think our family is stronger now than before we found her.

Courtney continues to reflect God's love for me by her being in my life these days. She just gave me a combination birthday-Mother's day present that is a little gold charm. I wear it around my neck; it reads, LIVE, LOVE, LAUGH. God has restored all those to me in the person of my daughter, Courtney.

                                          Alicia

SECTION III

HEARTCRIES OF HIS PEOPLE

"And the Lord said, I have surely seen the affliction of my people. . .and have heard their cry. . .for I know their sorrows"

Exodus 3:7

TIME WILL COME
By Mary Anne Manning Cohen

TIME WILL COME when our tragedy will not be replayed,
When no child will be torn out of the arms of love
    into the arms of money.
When all births will be blessed, all equal,
And there will be no word remembered to brand a child
    born outside society's ties, no recording of legal lies...
When love is more lasting than papers, and no child is
    deprived of either heritage or nurturing, even when
    they come from separate places.
And it is finally seen that blood and home are not the same,
And neither replaces the other,
    and there is no quota for love....

TIME WILL COME when social workers are to serve,
    not to sever;
When they know it is better to unite than separate,
To be true than to lie, to be seen than to hide,
To accept than renounce, that the giving and nurturing of life
    are both sacred and deserving of respect;
That all parents are real parents, not rivals.
That love is stronger than fear of laws or time, and cannot be
    terminated, cannot be legislated, cannot be denied...

TIME WILL COME when all children can grow, become real,
    cast off shadows, renew or sever ties by their own choice,
    be responsible, BE FREE!
When our bondage ends, and we answer to our children;
Answer with the gift of sight, gift of words, gift of sorrow...
When every person has the right to trace their roots in their
    mother's face, father's eyes...
When nobody is condemned to eternal childhood, and no
    mother cries forever...

THIS TIME MUST COME!

The Founding of Adoption Triangle Ministry

During the summer of 1980 I prayed a simple prayer. I prayed that God would use me and then show me what it was He wanted me to do with my life at that point in time.

I had become restless in my job and desired a change as well as a greater challenge. I was actively involved in the adoption movement holding various positions and offices over the previous five years. There was no doubt that I was sold out to the "cause", but there was something missing. I felt a strong desire to integrate my faith in some way--to bring my adoption experience and my Christian testimony together.

Within three days of that simple prayer, the seed for the Adoption Triangle Ministry was planted. I envisioned a set of birthparents, a set of adoptive parents, an adoptee and Jesus standing in a circle around the foot of the cross.

It became quite clear to me that the only kind of love that could break through the many barriers that had been built over the years was agape love--divine love--a love that is often beyond our human comprehension. Over the next several months, ATM began to take form.

My dear friends Charlene and David Justice shared in that early dream. Together we formed the purposes and goals –the main one being to bring the three parties together under the banner of God's love. Together we chose the motto "Where God and the Triangle Meet--There is the Fulness of

Love". We have all experienced aga*pe* love. We know the difference it can make in lives that are open to give it and receive it. We discovered, too, that our religious rituals could no longer cover the depth of the hypocrisy. We were kidding ourselves in trying to keep up a pretense that would protect us and/or our families. The game of "let's pretend" finally gave way as the billows of emotion began to pour forth. It was then we realized that only the truth would set us free.

ATM is dedicated to post-adoption services. We seek scriptural answers in dealing with such questions as "How does a birthparent come out of the closet and expose the hurts of the past and begin a healing process; how does an adoptee approach a found birthparent and/or deal with feelings of rejection; how does an adoptive parent deal with their threatened feelings of the search and help towards resolving their child's identity problems?"

ATM believes that everyone in the triangle is affected by the closed record system. ATM believes that most adoption agencies were founded on religious principles and that clergymen, doctors, and lawyers who were intermediaries in private adoptions usually did so with honorable intentions. However, due to a better understanding of the bond that unites us, we believe it is time for us to strive toward bringing about change.

ATM believes that the closed record system is unconstitutional and therefore goes against the very principles upon which our nation was founded, i.e. "We hold these truths to be *self-evident*, that all men are created equal, that they are endowed by their Creator with certain *inalienable* rights. . ." The word inalienable according to Webster means the inability to transfer. Yet isn't that what we've done when we falsify a document and call it legal in order to legitimize the adoptees' parentage? We've transferred their *birthright*!

In the second chapter of Exodus we clearly see that Moses sought out his kin and said to that present day system "let my people go". It is to that end that the following letters have been compiled. Some are responses to the 700 Club

Christian talk show my daughter, her adoptive mother, and I had the privilege of doing. Others are in response to the first book, but the majority have been sent to the Adoption Triangle Ministry. They are an expression of "our people", a people in bondage; not physical bondage as Moses' people were, but mental bondage - a bondage that stems from roots being severed.

Hopefully these letters will help to awaken the awareness of those who are in a position to institute change, and present them with a better understanding of what is going on in the minds and hearts of triad members. As only one of many spokespersons for the movement, and having personally shared in their heartache, I plead with our present day system to "let our people go".

Heartcries of His People

Dear ATM:

I recently read I WOULD HAVE SEARCHED FOREVER and very strongly identified with Sandy's account of her life and particularly her search. At the end, I felt I could have written it. I particularly appreciate her inclusion of her deep faith that God does have a hand directly in our affairs, and that His time is always perfect. I, too, am a deeply spiritual person and found it refreshing to read an account that did not hold back on pointing out God's mysterious way as He performs His wonders. Reading this book just reaffirmed my faith that if God closes one door there will always be others to open. I do believe in God's perfect timing, his absolute sovereign will, and I, on a rational level, know all things work together for good ultimately. However, on an emotional level, I just want to find my daughter, or at least get some important information passed on to her through the agency or whatever other means I can find.

At present I am very happily married to an attorney, who happens to be Jewish (and with whom

I, as a Christian, share a deep spiritual bond) and I have a son, 16, and a daughter 14. Both my children and husband support me in my search and are quite emotionally involved with it, themselves desiring it. So I am enjoying the full support emotionally of my family and do not have to be secretive about it. My mother and father-in-law also are behind me. My own parents are dead. My chosen profession is counseling all kinds of people in my role as psychologist and marriage, family, child counselor.

My father was an Assembly of God minister for over 50 years so I grew up in the church. As you may have heard, God has no grandchildren and my dad being a minister did not automatically make me a Christian. However, at a very young life, I dedicated my life to Christ. I am a "born-again, spirit-filled Christian". Being thus blessed does not insure one against the "fiery trials" and I have had countless tragedies, traumas, etc. the worst of which was having to give up my firstborn daughter. My life has been very transitory as well, having moved 47 times in the first 35 years of my life, experiencing a devastating divorce after 11 years of marriage (at which time my minister father treated me as if I were dead, it was abhorrent!!--even though my husband divorced me to marry my best friend). I then spent six years as a single parent, working to support us while I also went back to school and completed four years of college and then went on to complete graduate school and obtained my California State licensing.

Four years ago I met my husband-to-be, and we were married New Years Eve, 1976. The last five years have been the happiest of my life, and I look back on all the events that produced overwhelming sadness at times (twelve major deaths, together with my own clinical death twice along with three major surgeries) and while I was tempted often to cry out "WHY GOD???" I now look at my entire life and KNOW that there has been a purpose behind everything. I have a reputation for being an excellent therapist, and I feel this is due to my ability to identify with nearly every kind of problem clients come to me with, and I can truly say, I understand; I've been there, and I survived to enjoy that *abundant* life Christ came to provide us!

The singlemost traumatic event of my life has been the events surrounding the birth of my firstborn daughter and her subsequent relinquishment. Until just recently, through a series of events I feel were divinely inspired, I did not have any knowledge that I could search for my daughter. I was not aware of the whole adoption movement that is afoot, of which I am fast becoming an active part. I have had numerous people say to me they "KNOW" we will have a reunion. I personally have had above-usual psychic abilities and experiences which I think are nothing more than a higher spiritual awareness. Suffice to say at this point that I, too feel my daughter wants to find me, and is probably searching, and although I don't know the HOW of it, I feel the SURETY of our reunion one day. Still I find myself saying, Lord, I believe, help Thou my unbelief! Now and then when I run into roadblocks and closed doors, I just haven't come across the right door yet that will break my search, or perhaps she will find me first.

It is so strange (not really for us who believe) that in light of all the discouraging events, I still feel I am going to find her or vice versa. I just want to do anything and everything that I possibly can to expedite matters. My husband is an attorney, and an interesting little bit of guidance that I feel will come in handy some day is that I still go by my maiden name professionally. It was my identity for 17 years before I married Jim and my clientele and degrees and licenses are all under my maiden name, which was my name at the time I surrendered "Baby Girl" in May of 1961. For some strange reason, I have retained that name and identity (so she can find me?) and perhaps somewhere along the line in my search it will be useful to have my husband act as an intermediary on my behalf without being identified with me because of our different last names. He is also willing to drop everything and fly to New Jersey with me to assist in whatever capacity he can. He no doubt would be able to gain access to records that I could not just walk in and obtain. However, at this point I don't even know the court of jurisdiction where my daughter's adoption took place. This is one of the things I am asking the State of New Jersey to assist me in obtaining. They sent me a booklet listing all the agencies in New Jersey, both public and private, and I discovered residency requirements were in existence 18 years ago. This would narrow the search and court of jurisdiction to the counties listed in the state booklet for Children's Aid Society.

    I would greatly appreciate a reply and any suggestions you care to make. I think the counselor needs a counselor!! If you think it's worth it, I will hop the next plane to New Jersey and get with someone in person on my search. I've often wished I were wealthy these last few months so that I could just hop planes and go wherever I thought it might help.

    I appreciate your taking the time to read this, and anxiously (and prayerfully) await your reply.

M.B.

Dear Sandy:

I bought your book yesterday. I couldn't put it down. I loved it. I have so many people I want to read it. First on the list is my adoptive parents.

They knew my birthmother was looking for me 10 years ago. I was never asked how I felt about a meeting. I was a private adoption and raised two blocks from where she became pregnant. Everyone she asked that knew lied to her even though I was over 21.

My parents told me every so often of their friend who became obsessed with finding her mother and died in a snow storm searching. Also they always let me know it would break their hearts in two if I ever searched. I felt I owed them for all they had given me and it was the only way I could repay them by promising never to search.

Though I was 34 when she found me, they felt she should have contacted them first. Their answer to her would have been "It's none of your business --you gave all your rights up to her". I wouldn't have been told there was a contact.

The doctor told me when I was 18 that she had blonde hair and blue eyes. She has black hair and blue eyes. I was told I was Italian. I'm Scotch, Irish, French and German. This same doctor made promises to her which he never kept. She saw him every year begging for anything. I have seen the dated letters which she shared with me. The doctor died in 1970. At that time I felt there would be no way to ever find her.

Needless to say I was shocked when I received a call from my stepfather asking me if I knew I was adopted and telling me he thought he was married to my birthmother. They were at the door five minutes later. I had doubts until she gave me my father's picture. We are like two peas in a pod. On the back of a 34-year old photograph was his name and address. I called information and then made the call I always dreamed of. He responded with love.

As a child I was told over and over "If your mother loved you, she would have kept you." As a teen I remember feeling "How is anybody going to be able to love me when my own mother didn't." Seeing her, having her hold me, and five days of her sharing her life erased 34 years of doubt.

My adoptive parents are 70 and 73 and I do understand their fears. I feel that they are beginning to accept Fran's and mine relationship.

I thought I would always call her by name, but Mom just seems to come out sometimes. I WAS FOUND! I'm still on a high. I was with mom for two days in April and plan a week this summer so she can get better acquainted with her 10 year old granddaughter--her only grandchild.

Her whole family has accepted me. They have prayed for her for so long. She had nine brothers and sisters. Seven are living. I received a note from my 83 year old grandmother who is coming out to meet me in the fall. I am grateful also for my two half-brothers. Larry who is 33, retarded, crippled and epileptic said to me "I hope you like your brother half as much as he loves his new sister!" Jack, 30, is a bachelor who I'm crazy about. I was with him the morning his father died. His father signed my surrender papers.

On February 26th I was an only child and within a few days I discovered I had five sisters and four brothers.

My father's wife won't let him tell the children about me yet, though they're all grown. She was married to him when I was conceived and wouldn't give him a divorce. She has always known about me. I'v enclosed a letter from my Dad which I share with love. I could ask for no more.

Your daughter will grow in time. At 22 I would have been too immature to meet my birthmother. From 24 to 27 I had therapy which did wonders for me. Since then I have always put everything in God's hands. I let him worry for me.

My prayers are with you.

Love,

B.G.L.

A Letter of Love From a Found Birthfather to His Daughter

Dear B.G.,

You can't imagine how I longed to hear from you after your phone call which I wasn't given a chance to enjoy. I had nearly given up hope of ever knowing anything about you, but now I have a full heart and it feels great.

It's really hard to find words to express my feelings; your pictures tell me a lot, but I have a lot of questions. Yes, dear, you look like me very much and your birthmother never told me anything about you, or what had happened.

May God let me come to see you in the near future, be it His will. I visited Newport Beach in 1946, again in 1950, 1952 and 1954, but I had no name or any other information to go on. God knew best what to do and I'm glad to know you brought happiness to a lovely couple that could do so much for you at the time you needed it most.

You didn't say whether your adoptive parents

were still living or not. I hope that they are. Strange things happen in a lifetime and the years seem to fly by.

My wife is a wonderful woman and a patient and loving mother. Her name is Nellie May and she accepted Jesus as her Savior in 1946. I waited until 1958 to make my decision to live for Jesus. Have taught Sunday School and still do at this time and am an active deacon for the Brenton Baptist Church.

Now to tell you about your half brothers and sisters. . .Hope you are interested in knowing the above and I hope to send some pictures in the next letter to you.

B.G. you were a special gift from God and at a special time and may God keep on blessing the ones who love you so. I believe I remember them, but it has been a long time and many things have happened. Hold the picture of your mother. Nellie May is very jealous of her and with good reason. I don't like what she did to me and to you B.G., but I have been in love with her for 39 years now. Yes, I used the present tense and mean it, but I wouldn't hurt my loved ones here for anything. B.G. it has been a wonderful shock for me. When you asked me "do you know who this is?", I wanted to say my long lost daughter but I had quite a large audience at the time and wanted to protect them.

Nellie May is very old fashioned in her thoughts and ways and knows everyone in this small town. She was afraid the news would get out about you but I wouldn't care if the whole world knew about it. Will try to call if I get to a phone by myself long enough. Your call has been a blessing in many ways, but I hardly get a free minute alone any more. Please write again soon and remember that you have and always have had a special place in my heart, even though I have never seen you. Maybe some day I can prove it, until then, let's keep in touch.

****

A few months later

I love you, my first born, even though we have never met face to face. Your letters, pictures, and cards while on vacation are cherished and I hope to receive some more soon. Knowing about you has brought hope and happiness to my heart and I thank God that it happened. Nellie May doesn't think I should be proud of you but I am and feel like telling everyone about you. Enclosed is a picture of Nellie May and I taken this past year. Hope you will like it. She is resentful, but is trying to understand even though she doesn't want to share my love. We are all in good health and working regular and serving God as He leads us to do. B.G., being a Presbyterian, Baptist, Methodist, or any other denomination is not what counts with God. Having the *Love of Jesus* in our hearts and sharing that love with others is what really counts in our lives. Until later, I remain as always your earthly father, with a heart of love for you.

****

Dear ATM:

A friend of mine had been watching the 700 Club when Sandy Musser was interviewed. I think she was the mother or daughter who after some time of separation have found each other. I did not, unfortunately see the program. I wrote to the

700 Club for more information and they gave me this address.

I'm 32, never been married, although God has brought me a very beautiful evangelist to whom some day soon, I pray, we will be married. He, himself, has a little boy that was adopted. The boy lives with his ex-wife, but he has visiting rights.

I found the Lord in 1972, almost two years after I had given up my boy for adoption. The adoption agency I went through allowed me to see and hold him before he left the hospital to be with his new parents. I also wrote him a letter which his adoptive parents are to share with him when he reaches the right age. In the letter I tried to explain that I loved him and that under the circumstances it was best for him that I give him up for adoption.

After much prayer and seeking God concerning trying to find my son, God has confirmed that he has put this strong desire in me to do so. He is now ten years old. Would you send me any information you can in helping me to find him. I believe you are the channel God is using to help me. Please feel free to call me collect.

Thank you so very much. God's blessings of joy, love and peace be upon you and in you.

D.F.

****

Dear ATM:

I was so pleased to read of the new group you formed. I am a born again Christian adoptee desiring to know God's will in my search for my birthmother.

My adoption took place in Corvallis, Oregon, through a private doctor in 1954 when I was just an infant.

I am very unsure of how to handle this with my adoptive mother (my adoptive father is now dead). We have very rarely spoken of a possible search since it is such a sensitive subject and she is so easily hurt. She is not a Christian and I would choose until now not to tell her.

Now I am unsure which is best after reading letters in the CUB newsletter. Could I have some advice on this and also if you have any articles, etc. on how adoptive parents work out their feelings of threat.

Two years ago I wrote the doctor who delivered me and he was happy to give me my birthmother's first name and her town in Oregon that she was from. Our next step would be to visit the small town and check through high school year books for a maiden name.

Thanks for your help. I feel so thankful to the Lord for your work.

     In Christ's love

     L.S.

     ****

The following is the testimony of a birth grandmother presented at a legislative hearing in Missouri:

I have been present at this Model Adoption Act (meeting) approximately fifteen minutes. As it should be, those testifying express their views from a legal and emotional standpoint. My answer to the ideal adoption laws is to be guided by the awesome powers of love. Love does not hurt or betray. Love is faith, fulfillment, and survivorship.

I am a birth grandmother. To have open records in Missouri would be a dream come true. This is not a dream to reclaim the adopted child or alienate him from his adoptive family who loved and raised him to adulthood. They are and always will be the 'true parents.'

The birth family loses the child in a physical sense to the adoptive family, but the 'same' child remains forever in the heart of the birth family.

Within this sanctuary we spend much time with our child. We see him a healthy baby with one candle on his first birthday cake, catch him in protective arms when he takes his first faltering steps, and are proud of how handsome he is on his first day of school. This devoted vigil prevails a lifetime.

Cherished are our coveted priorities: we loved him first and gave him life.

To be realistic, we of the adoption triangle share an interdependence. There could no way be one side without the other.

Ideally, I like to think of the adoption triangle changing to the adoption *circle*, with the sharp angles of hurt, bitterness, and fear replaced with love, gratitude, and understanding.

It is discriminatory for adult adoptees to be denied their biological birth records. They are innocent of their birth circumstances and are deserving as legitimately born children. All are equal citizens.

May we of the Adoption Circle have compassionate hearts for each other and lovingly place the decision of the Model Adoption Act in the hands of the Supreme Judge--God, our heavenly Father.

With trusting heart, any replies to: A Birth Grandmother, P. O. Box 18033, Kansas City, Missouri 64133.

****

Dear Sandy,

I need help! You may remember me from some of the Philadelphia Adoption Forum meetings.

I surrendered a son for adoption in 1956--had pretty much managed to push under the painful feelings which only surfaced from time to time.

My birthson and I found each other through ALMA about a year ago. It was a great reunion-- and then "all hell" broke open for me. It was like the pain, guilt, and anger I had felt at the time of his surrender hit me full force, only doubly so, or maybe I've forgotten how bad I felt 24 years ago.

To make matters worse, my birthson hates me for giving him up for adoption. Well, I did the best I could but sometimes ones' best is not too adequate! He grew up in a broken home. He hardly ever saw his adoptive father, and when he was 16, his adoptive mother declared she was no longer his mother. What about the "perfect" home and parents we were promised for our children? Yet, I am a parent and I know I am not perfect-- and as a teenager, I don't think I would have been a very good parent.

I recently read a booklet on marriage--written by a priest--on the subject of "shotgun" marriages. He advised the young men--"Don't feel pressured to marry the girl--don't consider an abortion. Just see to it that the girl goes to a home for unwed mothers, where she will get help to "get her head on straight"--a "suitable" home will be found for the baby and gee whiz everything will work out okay." End of thinking on the subject!

Again I read a story about a man walking side by side with Christ on the beach. He could look back and see two sets of footprints in the sand. Suddenly a great trouble fell upon his shoulders and he could hardly bear the weight. He looked back and saw only one set of footprints and knew Christ had left him. Presently the man's burdens lightened and he again found Christ walking beside him--He asked Christ why he had deserted him in his time of trouble--Christ replied that indeed the man had not been deserted--that he had seen only one set of footprints because Christ had been carrying the man on his shoulders.

So I do feel rather deserted at the moment, but the Adoption Triangle Ministry makes a lot of sense to me.

Could you please send me more information--especially on ways I might become active--maybe if I can get myself straightened out, I might be able to help someone else.

F.H.

****

Dear ATM:

I am an adult adoptee who is currently engaged in a search for my birthparents. I recently attended an adoption conference at Drew University which is where I discovered your organization through your literature. I am also a born again Christian and very interested in your ministry. I would like to help you in any way that I could.

Before my children were born, I worked as an

adoption social worker. Of course, my ideas and opinions have changed a great deal over the course of time and I still have a great deal to learn about the dynamics of the adoption triad.

Recently I obtained the name of my birthmother. I'm quite excited about that although I realize I still have a way to go before actually locating her. However, now I feel that reunion is a real possibility, and it is a little scary. I am a member of ALMA and they have been very helpful in my search, but I would really love to have some scriptural answers to some of my feelings and questions. So I would be most interested in attending any group discussions or workshops you may be planning.

Enclosed please find a small donation. I would be happy to donate my time in any way that you think I could be helpful. In the meantime I would appreciate any literature that you could refer me to. Thank you!

C.M.

****

Six Months Later:

Thank you for your note, and for the five tracts I just received. I will be sending for some copies of them in the near future. There are two or three of us triangle members here who are talking about getting together and starting some kind of meetings, but we need a little direction.

I hope by September to have my life back into some sort of order. A great deal has happened since I last wrote to you. At the end of March, I had a very warm and positive reunion with my birthmother, two half sisters and a half brother. I was very warmly received and accepted, but it was a very emotionally straining experience. I was flying high for a month and then my adoptive mother died on April 3. Praise God, without His strength and comfort I could not have handled it all. I feel very strongly that the Lord led me to my birthmother and family (it was too "flukey" the way I found them). That belief has helped to minimize the guilt I felt when my adoptive mother died. She never knew about my search and would not have understood or accepted it at all. I trust that the Lord has explained it all and that she understands now what she could not have in life.

I feel very committed to helping other members of the triangle to a greater understanding, openness and acceptance of each other. From my own experience, I relize that only God can heal all of the hurt, guilt, bitterness, and resentment that the adoption experience can result in. I'm so grateful that I knew the Lord and He was with me through it all. In Him, I have found the unconditional love, acceptance, and security that we all crave.

I still have my depressed days when everything just seems too confused and too much-- (The Lord still has a lot of work left to do on me.) So let me know if you have any meetings planned or if you can give us any direction.

                In Christs' love,

                C.M.

                ****

Dear Sirs:

A friend of mine recently told me about a guest speaker you had on the 700 Club during the late part of April or early May who was interested in helping adopted children to locate their real parents.

Please do not think I'm upset about being adopted because I'm not, but the Lord has led me recently to pray for my real parents and I have, but since praying I have been really concerned for my real mother. I really truly want for her to know that I am well and alive and that she is a grandmother of three fine boys.

I love my adopted parents and I have led a beautiful life thanks to them. However, my father was Jewish and in his 40's and my mother was Roman Catholic in her thirties and in 1944 there were very strict laws about adoption. This adoption procedure was done privately through attorneys who are all dead now and I've reached dead ends everywhere, including attorneys who won't even get a little involved. I do not wish to cause anybody any embarrassment but I do feel being led by the Lord to write this letter. Please if possible refer this letter to someone who can help me.

Very sincerely in Jesus,

R.Mc

****

Dear Sister-in-Christ,

I received your information about the Adoption Triangle Ministry and I was so pleased to know of such a work and witness for the Lord.

I have completed my search almost three years ago now and because I have a very large new family, it is taking me some time to meet them. As I review my pilgrimage in this matter, I can see the clear hand of God in various ways, and in a few matters, especially in the search, there were dramatic and powerful events.

I now see that God will use my experience to minister to others as he has been doing here in the Vancouver area and if I can be of any further help in seminars, etc., I am open to serve in this way. I am presently collecting for a paper on "Support Systems For Adoptees."

I was encouraged to note your goals and methods for the ministry and I would be most willing to share my material from the B.C. scene as it relates to your goal and procedures. We have really only begun here, but I am thankful for what has been accomplished to this point.

May the Lord richly bless you as you serve Him in this ministry.

Sincerely in Christ,

J.R., Minister
B.C., Canada

****

Dear Mrs. Musser:

I have just finished reading your book and I must say it has left me with many questions and mixed emotions.

I am an adoptee nearing my 30th birthday and I feel that now is the time to begin my search for my birthmother. I accidently learned of my adoption at the age of nine years. Since then I have been in almost constant emotional turmoil wondering who I really am. The ironic thing is that I was born and adopted in the same city. My birthmother and adoptive parents all lived in the same city. So you see, I am so close, yet so far from the information I need.

After learning of my adoption I felt nothing but bitterness and hatred for the woman who "surrendered" me. It wasn't until I was married and had children of my own that my feelings toward her changed. Loving my children the way I do I still couldn't understand how someone could give up her own flesh and blood. But now I'm more open to the probability that there was a good reason.

When my second child was born in 1979 with birth defects, I contacted the Social Services Department to inquire about my medical history. The social worker contacted my birthmother's sister and was able to give me much of the information I requested. She also gave me information regarding the circumstances of my conception, my birthparents' physical characteristics and even updated information about my birthmother and her present family. My birthmother's sister even spoke of her desire to meet me.

And now my reason for writing to you is to ask for your help in beginning my search. If you could just tell me how and where to begin, I would greatly appreciate it.

Both of my adoptive parents are now deceased so I feel I can devote much time and energy to this search, without fear of hurting those who loved me so deeply.

I must admit that I fear rejection because I feel

that my birthmother has had equal time to search for me. I just hope that some day we will meet and all my questions will be answered. She has two beautiful grandchildren. It will be her misfortune if she never meets them.

Thank you for taking time to read this letter. I would deeply appreciate any help or advice you could give me. I feel that my search is about to begin.

Most sincerely,

S.D.

****

Dear Sandy,

I just recently finished reading your book and now I find that you are the founder of ATM. When I first read of your group in the "Log" I was thrilled. I'm so glad to find a Christ-centered support group. I intend to suggest we tithe to your group. We are in need of money, therefore we need to plant some seeds.

Please send me every little bit of information about ATM as I am constantly being told that my need to know who I am is a spiritual illness. Our other Christian adoptees and birthparents face this same attack. You know, the world never hurts us the way the body of Christ can (or maybe I should say other Christians).

I go before the judge on June 30, hopefully to get my birthmother's name. Please pray God's will be done. I believe His will is my heart's desire. Also pray she will want me. I need her so badly as she is all I have (almost). I am prepared for the truth whatever it is, though. My little girl is also adopted. I hope I am paving the way for her. I don't wish for her to go through what I've been through. Please let me hear from you soon. God bless your work!

>Love in Jesus

>M.S.

>****

Dear Sandy,

My how time flys when one leaves their direction to the Lord's guidance. Sometimes He keeps me so busy, my head swims.

Your particular ministry excites me. How is it being received? I would be happy to speak as an adult adoptee who tried the courts and but by the "Grace of God" survived my "ordeal". Learned much from it. Still have to write a book! The Lord has not provided for that yet. I'm waiting. I'm learning so much that He may want my story to tie into my six year work with the adoption triangle.

Please send me any and all information on your "new group", pamphlets, scripture relationships—the whole thing. I'm enclosing a check to help defray mailing costs.

Bless you so much for doing His work. As the plaque on my kitchen wall says "Tho we get weary working for the Lord, the benefits are out of this world"! God Bless you—I pray for you often.

>Love,

>M. Maul
>Founder of A.I.M.
>Orchard Park, N.Y.

Dear Sandy,

I'm so glad I got to meet you. I had read your book a couple months ago and it was exciting to put a personality with it. You've had so many emotional experiences in your life, it is wonderful that you are willing to share them to help others.

I wanted to tell you a story that has always meant a lot to me. I searched for my birthmother for ten months. During that time there were three or four occassions when I just did nothing with my search for a few weeks. One of those times was in October of 1979 when I was busy preparing for a Renewal (a two day retreat) at our church. Up until that Renewal weekend I would call myself semi-religious, only needing God on occassions. On that weekend there was a most beautiful song used over and over again that was taken from Isaiah 49. I heard you quote it, so I know you are familiar with it. I wasn't sure if anyone else heard the words, but I became convinced the song was written for me. It was God's way of telling me to continue with the search, that my birthmother wouldn't reject me. At that point I was sharing with very few people about my search because so many people just don't understand.

After being a participant on the Renewal in October, we were invited to form a team to spend six months preparing to give a Renewal in April of 1980. I found myself at a "history giving" meeting in November telling the group of nineteen strange women my life's story and tearfully explaining my emptiness at not knowing my birth family. We spent six months praying together and getting to know one another and I rather quietly continued with my search. I had been asked to witness which meant giving a 20 minute talk about "He Extends

Love Perpetually." It was filled with many voids in my life from not knowing my birth family. An intermediary spoke with my birthmother on March 27, 1980 and she wrote to me in April. I promptly called her and we had a beautiful phone conversation for two hours on April 25–the day before the Renewal started.

My team did not know this until my witness and with my own tears so strong that I could barely speak, mixed with the tears of 40 women in one room, I shared with them how God had allowed me to know a very special woman.

Sandy, it was one of the most beautiful things that ever happened to me as an adult. God and I are now true, loyal, wonderful friends on a daily basis.

Best wishes in all your work.

Love,

P.B.

****

Dear Sandy,

I so personally relate to your book, *I Would Have Searched Forever,* because of the deep personal sharing and the added spiritual dimension.

I own a Christian Book Store so Logos sent this as a sample, but I also had heard through a newsletter from Massachusetts that you went through a period of time just sending cards, a note, etc. to your daughter and after three years her return for a relationship.

As an adoptee, I've written an article of my own that I've shared with several denominational papers, none of which feels it is a subject they can "touch". I am sure you are finding as I have that every publisher doesn't even want to touch this subject. I am so glad that Logos did. Brother Malachuk has been a real leader in the Charismatic movement and I received Logos from the very first issue back in '66 or '67. It has been a real strength to me.

That's why I'm enclosing the article and the actual letter I wrote to my birthmother. I don't want you to just have to wade through one more reunion, for they are all so personal and yet so precious to each of us. I am trying to help those I deal with here to realize the spiritual impact and that there is a need to deal in this area regardless of what denominational background you come from.

My mother while thrilled to know me, is married to the man I strongly believe is my father though it has never been proven and they tell me it can't be for sure. There was another man in her life for a period of six weeks while he was away and I have an older brother, two younger brothers and a sister who she feels she can't share with and is terribly afraid they will find out. I am sending her your book and praying that will open the way for her to understand. We in the large cities don't understand what it is like to live in a community of about 200 people that don't change and to this day would well remember the whole situation and me since I was no "secret".

Would you pray for her and if there is anything you might share because she feels I'll have no relationship with them because of the age difference.

I would like to get information about the "ministry" aspect of the Adoption Triangle. I lost my adoptive father who was 77 the day before

Thanksgiving and my mother is not well. I am active in a group and talk with different people, but to some extent I am still in a closet because I have an adoptive mother that I know could not cope.

I have ordered 25 copies of your book to distribute--some I'll brown bag and mail anonomously to those I know would benefit from your story. I know the Lord really led in my reunion and it is in this aspect that we totally relate to each other now. She needed my forgiveness and to know that I held nothing against her. She felt her "salvation" was not complete until we talked and prayed together.

She was thrilled when I named my second child for her. I wish you would pray with us that her heart would be opened to telling her children, not only for my deep desire, but that the truth will totally set her free so she can walk again with a head held high and community gossip won't bother her.

Thanks so much for giving us the Christian perspective.

Sincerely,

L.P.

****

Two Weeks Later - February 20, 1981

Your letter and information came just as you were introduced on the 700 Club. I was glad that Ben interviewed you, but only wish you had been given more time. Cindy's mom did a beautiful job as an adoptive mother--the subject seems to be a "time bomb" type.

In my own case, besides by adoptive mother being sick, all my life she has tried to destroy whatever I do. In the "religious" community here I am widely known having been raised in a strong Baptist home and also worked closely with the "charismatic renewal".

For me to be involved in a ministry, to some extent I would have to be in the "shadows" because of the volatile person my adoptive mom is. I can, however, write and talk to people (as long as I'm out of my local area churchwise--I can pretty much say and do what I like). Adoption to her is "ownership".

My birthmom is great but I won't and can't jeopardize anything there either. As long as I do things in a discreet way she has no objection, but I never set out to hurt or destroy her privacy or family life in any way. Perhaps you relate, but being a "city slicker", I don't understand or comprehend rural life and social standards. She's in an area of 200 people and has never lived elsewhere since she was 13 and all this happened when she was 21. She's reading your book, but since she's on an eight party line to complicate things, we don't discuss it on the phone. She's a doll and in my case I want to be closer, but the Lord will work it out in *His* time. I have to trust that.

I am excited and cautious because I have to be where God wants me and I must stay in the center of His Perfect Will.

God's best to you. I've got ten copies of your book circulating so we'll see what happens.

****

Dear Sandy,

I just received my copy of CUB Communicator (CUB's newsletter). When I opened to page two I knew a prayer had just been answered. I am a very grateful birthmother, who by the grace of God, is able to have some contact with my son after 27 years.

He called me Easter Sunday, April 1980. We had a reunion in May. I have talked with his adoptive mother on the phone and we have written to each other. My son lives in North Carolina and I live in Massachusetts so we try to enjoy a relationship via the mail and phone. I am sure he wants this. However, I feel so much guilt that I am unable to enjoy this special relationship. I am sure the answers to my problems with this are in scripture. Would you please send me information about the Adoption Triangle Ministry. I'll be waiting to hear from you.

A.C.

****

Dear Sandy, (from an adoptive mother)

Thanks for writing back to me and sharing some insights into CUB. I sincerely appreciate knowing about CUB and what it's doing for birthparents, not just for my own interest, but for a help to our son, Jim, when he may reach the time in his life when he may feel the need to contact his birthparents.

I have to be honest with you. I was just as scared and confused about the possibility of Jim being contacted or Jim doing the contacting of his birthparents some day as many other adoptive parents have been in the past. It was through a very tragic experience shortly after we adopted him that "my eyes were opened" as well as my heart. I became pregnant shortly after we adopted Jim. I went into labor ten weeks premature and our son only lived for one day. We were shattered.

Within a nine month span we had gone through all the emotional upheavels of an adoption, parenting, a pregnancy and death. I shiver just thinking back now to that time in my life. Fortunately, we had some terrific support from a dear friend and from our God. During this time the seed was planted of what a birthparent goes through after separation from their child--whether it be right away or in years to come. Some of these insights were shared with me by a gal who had "surrendered" her baby.

I began to feel somewhat like a birthparent myself. I had gone through a fairly normal pregnancy and then my baby was taken away. Although I knew where my baby went, the fact was still there–he wasn't with me. I'd never get to hold him. I'd never get to see him smile for the first time. I'd never hear him say "Mommy, I love you." I knew he was being cared for and I knew heaven was a much better place for him. But I still felt cheated and alone. To me, this has to be much of what a birthmother must feel too. She's been told her baby is being cared for and is in a better place, but many times she feels cheated and alone.

My heart cried out for my son's birthmother on the day I wrote him the poem. I was frustrated. I wanted her to know so much that he was doing just fine and that we love him so very much. I wanted to thank her for giving life to him and not ending it before it even started. I hope this makes sense to you. This is very hard for me to share on paper without it sounding a bit empty.

Thanks for giving me the opportunity to share these feelings with you.

S.W.

This is the poem that is referred to in the above letter:

A BIRTHDAY

It's my child's birthday today
He just went dashing by me
His eyes are sparkling with the excitement
    only meant for today
Presents, kisses, hugs, cake, ice cream—
It all seems so natural
It's a day for looking back and looking forward.

It's my child's birthday today
But there's something very different happening inside of me
This should be a day of complete joy
A day for thanksgiving
But I'm stopped in the midst of all this excitement
I'm stopped because my thoughts are with "someone" else
    for a time.

It's my child's birthday today
I have no memories of the pain and struggle,
    as he entered this life
As he fought for his first breath
I have no memories of his life growing inside of me and
    fighting to be released
I have no memories from the beginning months of his life
Another "someone" was there—Another "someone"
    suffered for my joy.

*It's my child's birthday today
But "someone", somewhere, is feeling an emptiness inside.
I wonder if she is wondering—*
> *Wondering who he looks like
> Wondering how big—how small
> Wondering if he laughs much
> Wondering if he will wonder someday too.*

*It's my child's birthday today
And in the middle of this blessed day that was given to me
I have a prayer.*
> *Oh God, that I may never forget that "someone" suffered so much to give life to my child. That "someone" loved my child so very much in that she gave him the right to live. May I never forget for a moment and especially now, today, to offer a prayer of thanks for that "someone" and that you, dear God, can always be there by that "someone" to help her through the hurts she will have when she stops to think that today is "My child's birthday". Amen.*

*—from an adoptive mother,
Sue Westrum, Glenville, MN*

Dear Ms. Musser:

    I have for many years known the name and location of my son, keeping my deep dark secret, feeling that I would have to wait until eternity to be united. I have always been, and still am, fearful of what it might do to him, his adoptive parents, and myself, if I would intervene. He is now 31 years of age; I am 56 and never married.

    On several occasions when he was a child and was in the same city, I would have someone, who did not know the purpose, drive me past his house through which I learned he had a dog. Also on one occasion, coincidently and unbelievably, I dined with someone who knew the family, which I discovered through conversation, and you can imagine the secret anxiety I experienced. Through a few discreet questions, I learned a little about the family.

    Throughout the years, I have prayed for him and about possibly being united with him. However, for 36 years I worked as a secretary until I sustained a fracture last year and only through being home, was I able to view the telecast and learn of you.

    The name I am using is a shortened form of my official name on the birth certificate; it has occurred to me that had he searched for me, this may have been an obstacle.

    At this writing, for reasons mentioned above, I hesitate about taking action. It will be interesting to learn your response. I have a close association with the Lord and pray that I will be guided.

                      B. E. S.

****

Dear Sandy:

My husband and I own a Christian bookstore here in New Port where we receive all new releases from publishers. Praise God for your book! I haven't put it down since it arrived last week. You see, I too am a birthparent. My son was born 2/28/71 in Chicago, Illinois. I was 19. He was adopted when he was 11 days old. His birth certificate says "Baby Boy", but I've always called him Stephen Daniel. He just celebrated his 10th birthday. I think about him every day of my life and wonder if he's dead or alive - wonder what color his hair is and wonder what color his eyes are; how big he is, and then I wonder if he understands why I gave him up for adoption. I did leave a letter with the adoption agency to be given to him, but I don't know whether he ever got it.

I come from a Christian family and it was "decided for me" that adoption was the best for me and my son, and afterwards "I could forget and go on with life." But I think you know that is not always so easy to do. I've kept this inside of me for over 10 years now and it was so refreshing to read your book and find out that other people feel as I do!

May God bless you richly for what you have meant in my life, even though I don't know you personally and may He bless your endeavors with ATM. I'm so thankful for your book and that it crossed my path. Thank you, Sandy.

E. H.

****

Dear Sandy:

I am a birth aunt and also an adult adoptee. My story is not any different than most adoptees. I was surrendered for adoption at birth, but last year I started my search. I was born in upstate New York and raised there until 1965 - after my marriage, we moved to my husband's hometown. I am married with four children.

Because of my childrens' medical problems, I decided to search. My 16 year old is an epileptic and one of our sons is asthmatic. The other one is borderline cystic. My other daughter and I have audible heart murmurs. So you see why I couldn't understand information being withheld (I also had three stillborn babies).

After starting my search I accidentally found out that I had two sisters. For me it was a sign from God to hang in there and to move heaven and earth in locating them. It was with His power and love that guided me throughout the search. I have located one sister and she also is the birthmother to my neice. The girl - who was born on my birthday is still too young to know or probably unaware of my existance or the problems in society today. This type of criteria keeps me actively involved in the Triad.

With your love of God and your birthdaughter, I am sure He will reward your efforts trifold. God has always taught reconciliation and love to all - but so few people take advantage of it. It was through my search that He taught me Love, Patience and Forgiveness. And I will continue to feel and give this feeling to all I touch; especially to adoptive parents. They must know and come to the understanding that as birthparents and adoptees we only want to make the love they have given to us known to All in All ways. Forgiveness, Happiness & Love are the three strongest words I know - as well as Love of God.

K.L.

****

Dear Ms. Musser:

Having recently found my natural father, I am now trying to understand why it became so important to me. I was told by the Triadoption Library in Westminster, California that you are familiar with Biblical teachings on the subject, and of the importance of blood-line in general.

I am interested primarily in the point of view of the adoptee, but also that of the natural parent (my father is an alcoholic and would drink more heavily near my birthday), and also of the adoptive parent(s), or in this case, the step-parent. My mom is my natural mother, but she and my father divorced when I was a baby. She consequently married my dad when I was two, and I was adopted by him when I was four. There must have been a lot of bitterness toward my father, because I was twelve before they told me, and even then they almost didn't. (The courts had changed my birth certificate, so that made Dad my "physical" father as well). My mother never talked to me about him, although she offered to answer any questions I might have. The few times I did, I could see it was traumatic for her, and I concluded he must have been an awful man and since I was born five months after their marriage, I must have been a terrible mistake.

I also felt that to even *think* about it would be

a betrayal to my family. Eventually, none of these things mattered. I felt I *had* to find him before my birthday once the decision was made, and I had just three days. It took two. (I have yet to understand the emotional forces that *compelled* me to find him). I met him the day before my 26th birthday.

I really like my natural father - and there was an immediate bond. It thrilled me to know how much I look like him! My parents do feel betrayed, and there are many unresolved problems, but I feel more complete somehow. *Just what is the bond?*

Some other questions I have are: 1) What compels an adoptee to search out a natural parent despite the fears? 2) I almost felt like I was searching for my own identity - perhaps roots or heritage. Why? 3) Why does a birthday hold such importance? 4) Why do step-parents or adoptive parents feel so betrayed? and 5) What is the Biblical importance of blood-line? (Much of the Bible is devoted to "begets", and the blood-line to Jesus seems to be very important). Any literature you could recommend would probably be very helpful.

C.J.

****

Dear Ms. Musser:

I am an adoptive mother who is in full sympathy with your group.

Our daughter will be sixteen in a few weeks and I hurt for her and her "birthmother".

Whenever I am with my mother, my daughter is miserable for a day or two afterwards. "You look so much like your mother, who do I look like?"

Now that she is preparing for an art career, she would love to discuss her talent with the person whose artistic genes she carries.

I have written to the director of our adoption agency in Long Beach requesting his help should inquiries be made by her mother.

My husband and I are quite secure in our parenthood but we know there is another dimension to our daughter and she will never be fulfilled until they meet.

Our 18 year old son has not indicated a desire at this point. We have kept photos of all stages of growth in the event they should meet one day.

As we were leaving the agency with our son I said to our caseworker, "Now, at age 21 he will be supplied with the information to find his parents, won't he?" She almost jumped out of her skin and then laid the guilt trip on us -- "If you do a good job, they won't ever want to know!"

I certainly hope that one day soon our daughter finds the roots she longs for. I want to meet her also. After all, she has been a silent member of our household for almost 16 years.

Sincerely,

Adoptive Parents

****

The following is the *only* negative letter I've received and it's from a "Christian brother".

I am writing you as an adopted child (now an adult) *and* as a parent who has adopted a child.

I am in sympathy with your situation in that I can understand the guilt you must have experienced over those many years after giving your child away - for adoption. I am glad that you found Christ, and that your life has changed. But at the same time I *strongly* do not believe that gives you the right to come back 20 years later (or however long it was) and try to force or interject yourself into other people's lives and create new problems for them. I think that is very selfish on your part and that when you gave up the child - you also gave up all your rights as a mother to that child.

I was adopted. I think of the person who gave me birth as only that - a person who gave me birth. She was never, and has never been a mother to me. My mother and father are the gracious people who took me into their home at a very early age, clothed me, fed me, raised me, gave me principles to live by, took care of me when I was sick, and did all the other things that parents do for their children. They are my parents, have always been and will always be.

The lady who gave me birth tried to find me (and finally did) some years back, after I was married. I really did not want to see her or have any kind of relationship with her. She was just like another person to me - nothing special at all. My parents were honest with me and told me about the situation and asked me if I wanted to meet her. I told them not really, but if it would help her and maybe ease her guilt, I would do it.

A meeting was set. I felt nothing. I looked at a pitiful woman who had paid a great price for her actions of the past and had regretted it for many years. I felt pity for her, but that's all. I saw her and my sister (whom I had never seen before) a few more times and then decided to break off the contact because I felt there was no point or reason for it to continue. I really felt for my parents. I knew what they were feeling and how this was affecting them. They never once tried to persuade me *not* to see this lady. I decided this on my own and I have never regretted it for one moment.

You came on the PTL show to air your views on this matter. You are entitled to your opinion, but that's as far as it goes where I am concerned. I disagree with you. I think you are wrong. I came away with the impression that you were selfish and expected FAR TOO MUCH from the situation YOU had created quite a few years ago. We've all sinned. We all have regrets. We all live with guilt from time to time. And - we're all responsible for our sins and our mistakes and cannot expect to choose our own consequences.

Again, I say, I am glad you are now a Christian. Your sins, like ours, have been forgiven and are under the blood of Jesus Christ. But this does *not* give you the right to impose your thoughts, your desires, your problems on other innocent people who have just tried to do their best to raise the child.

They too, have feelings and hopes and dreams and desires - and - RIGHTS!

I am sorry if I seem to be so against what you said on PTL. But from my standpoint as an adopted child and as an adoptive parent my position is opposite from yours. When you gave up the child - you gave up ALL rights to that child and his or her future.

I wish you the best in the Kingdon of God. I pray He blesses you beyond all measure. I pray His grace will be sufficient for you. But I do not pray that you have a relationship with the girl you gave birth to. That is not your right.

Sincerely,

N.B.

I wrote and thanked him for sharing his thoughts with me. I also thanked him for the prayers on my behalf and that I, too, was praying for him - that the Lord would give him compassion and love for the woman who gave him a special gift - life!

****

In conclusion, those of us active in the movement are drawn to certain people who are having difficult searches, and for whom we would do almost anything if we could "break the case." Bob Wickboldt is one of those people who has crossed my path. We met in Louisiana at a conference sponsored by the Adoptees Birthright Committee. I found his story to be so fascinating and frustrating that I share it in the hope of a breakthrough. It begins with a letter from his mother. The letter had been in the agency file and was given to him when he began his search. It is dated June 29, 1944 and begins "My darling son:

> If you only knew how very much I want to see you and hold you close. Sweetheart you are everything to me. I am working night and day so that I can pay the money I owe and have you my son forever. I hope you are well.
> I dreamed an awful dream about you. Don't let anything happen to you. You and I are all each other have.
> Momee loves you darling, without you life could not go on. You and I have had a pretty rugged life your 2 short years. But we will have some breaks.
> I have prayed every nite for God to help us and by my doing the right thing He is going to help us. I am coming for you as soon as I get paid. I get paid on the 5th.
> Darling don't have forgotten me. You will soon be having a 2nd birthday.

It seems that you know too how nobody wanted you, and how almost alone we were except for Elizabeth, and remember how my sister (your auntie) came because I was her only sister and that I had disgraced the family and had to be told every day.

The long wait before you were born was hard. I was staying with Aunt Evelyn and remember how ashamed she was for her friends to see me.

I talked to you then as I am talking now and I think you have understood from the beginning. By the grace of God and by your standing by, we are going to have a little home some day.

Since the day I knew or the day Dad knew I have not had a home and, since you came, neither have you.

Remember, our staying in the hospital 15 days because we had no one to take us home with them, and then dear Aunt Evelyn took us but siad she would not wait on us and that I would have to get out as soon as I was able to work.

I never went to bed when I came from the hospital. I stayed up all day every day, washed yours and my clothes, helped mop, clean yards, anything, until you were five weeks old and we - you and I - rented a two-room upstairs apartment. With the little pieces of furniture we could get together, we started living there.

I got a little colored girl to look after you and I went to work. You were only five weeks old. I remember how that I worked all day and came home and you and I stayed together at night.

We were happy. Then you were sick with cold and you seemed to almost choke at times and I would sit up all night afraid to go to sleep, not wanting to go to sleep because darling we were one and are still one.

And then came Col. Revere all the way from Eglin Field with Capt. Nauman. The Col., then a Major, telling me how much he loved us and wanted us with him, not telling me he was still married.

I wanted the best for you "Butch" so we went.

He was still married and his wife and son living with him. I went to work leaving you with the lady he got for us to live with. Everything was going all right until he began telling people (while drinking) that you were his and that he loved us. Then when he was sober and knew that he had talked too much, he and this same Capt. Nauman said that you and I were the ones to leave so they packed us up and took us to Crestview and put us on a train.

From that day till this, we have been pushed around. We were happy just the two of us and the little Negro girl who cried when we left and they persuaded us away.

Darling, don't forget your mother (momee). I love you. You don't know how much I ache for you now and wonder if you are all right.

Good night for now, my darling.

> Your Momee

Bob learned from the social worker that his mother was 17 years old when he was born and his father was an Air Corps officer. But there is still so much that does not make sense. It is clear from the letter, however, that she fully intended to get her son on July 5, when she got paid. What happened to her? Did she die? If she did, why wasn't he placed for adoption immediately.

He became a ward of the state, drifting from foster home to foster home, spending much time living in the French Quarter. He recalls those years that made him street-wise. His earliest memories are of roaming the streets of the

French Quarter, shining shoes in bars and sleeping behind bushes along the streets.

Through the clues in the letter, Bob did trace his father hoping to get some information on his mother. His father had died. He spoke with his father's widow who was the second wife. She said that she vaguely remembered her husband speaking of a young woman and baby, but that was all.

Bob is naturally feeling a lot of anger toward the people who were involved with his mother, because of their obvious lack of concern for her. He believes she may have had a strong feeling that something was going to happen to him - or her. The fact that he was illegitimate could have hurt his father's military career, as well as his family, since they were involved in Louisiana politics. Obviously, he was under a lot of pressure.

Since I still believe in miracles I am claiming one for Bob! Bob has just recently learned the name of his mother.

SECTION IV

ILLEGAL, IMMORAL, AND FATTENING

The agencies, the courts, the doctors, and the adoptive parents, faced with the eventuality that facts formerly hidden will be revealed, will have to substitute candor for concealment and honesty for distortion. The effects will ripple backwards to free adoptees still in childhood from adult pretense.

> Linda Burgess, Author
> *The Art of Adoption*

An Inalienable Right

"We hold these truths to be self-evident, that all men are created equal, that they are endowed by their Creator with certain *inalienable* rights...the right to life...liberty... and the pursuit of happiness."

These words, of course, originate at the birth of our country. They are a symbol of our guarantee that everyone in our country will be treated just and equal. But our lawmakers of the 40's developed the present adoption laws which take away those basic rights from the very group of people the adoption system was meant to serve! They developed a system that actually does exactly what our constitution says cannot be done--transferred the rights of the adoptee. How? By denying them the right of liberty to choose whether or not to seek their natural heritage. If their pursuit of happiness happens to involve the decision to search, they are denied this right as well, since the present laws exclude an adopted person from ever knowing his own personal heritage.

Whether the present adoption laws were developed with good intentions of anonymity for the birthparents, protection of the adoptee, or security for the adoptive parents, it is certainly time for us to realize and accept that these things are no longer in the best interest of any of the parties to adoption.

Adoptees must know their background and heritage to

complete the how and why of their existence. Birthparents must know that the child they loved and surrendered to adoption is alive, well, and happy, and thereby begin to ease the pain in their lives. And finally, the adoptive parents must be relieved of the burden of carrying a secret that fosters feelings of resentment, fear, and insecurity.

David vs. Goliath

It's been said that the meek shall inherit the earth - if they can mount an effective lobbying effort! At the first American Adoption Congress conference in Washington, D.C. the following resolution was passed:

"Open records complete with all identifying information for all members of the adoption triad, birthparents, adoptive parents and adoptee at the adoptee's age of majority *or earlier* if all members of the triad agree." (May 6, 1979).

It was not until I attended the conference in Kansas City in 1981 that I realized that we are indeed in battle over this issue. The National Committee for Adoption (NCFA) had representatives there candidly sharing their "strategy" of keeping the records closed and that their "target areas" would be those states with pending open records legislation. Apparently from the strong use of war terms, they were armed and ready to attack any efforts we were making. Goliath had a budget for the first years' operation of $200,000. This financial giant's support came from fifteen private agencies!

The agencies supporting the NCFA are mostly private agencies which in turn are largely funded by churches and adoptive parent groups. Then I recently learned that the Moral Majority is also against open records! My immediate thought was "What is moral about keeping someone's heritage and birthright locked up forever?"

There is absolutely nothing in scripture that alludes to adoption the way it is handled in this country today. Therefore, it's difficult for me to understand the "Christian" thought that supports closed records. Moses had, for all intents and purposes, an open adoption. It is extremely clear from the written text that his own birthmother was his nursemaid. We know that he had a natural longing for his kin, and his geneology is clearly stated in the sixth chapter of Exodus for all to see.

Under the present system, we are still practicing what the prophet Micah suggested when he said "Shall I give my first-born for my transgression, the fruit of my body for the sin of my soul?" (Micah 6:7) Isn't that what we've required of the woman carrying an "out-of-wedlock" child? We've coerced them into giving up their first-born in order to pay for their transgression - the fruit of their body for the sin of their soul! We've made them feel guilty and convinced them that this was the right thing to do. This would be her punishment for the sin committed; a lifelong separation from her first-born child - never to know anything about him. Even our hardened criminals receive a pardon or reprieve after a certain length of time - but not our birthparents. Their suffering and punishment is intended to go on forever - the punishment to fit the crime! As one mother expressed it, "Adoption is the only paper you sign that comes with a life sentence."

Take note that the above mentioned scripture is posed as a question. The verse following that one responds with another question and then the answer. "What does the Lord require of you? To do justly, to love mercy, and to walk humbly with your God." (Micah 6:8) Certainly that verse is full of love, forgiveness, understanding, and compassion; not punishment and judgment.

It is a sad but true commentary that "Christians are the only ones who kill their wounded," even though it's been 2,000 years since Jesus said, "Let him that is without sin cast the first stone."

The Case of the Missing Open Records Section

The Health and Human Services Model Adoption Act appeared in the October, 1981 issue of the Federal Register. The Open Records Section had been omitted. Why? Could it be that pressure from powerful opponents and/or articles like the following effected the deletion? One headline read: SOCIAL PLANNERS PROPOSE ANTI-FAMILY ADOPTION REFORM and listed what they consider to be three main dangers of the proposed Model Adoption Act Open Records Section.

1) Increased problems for adoptive families and relinquishing families;
2) Create severe social and emotional problems;
3) Adoptions through agencies would decline in number.

Not one of these points mention the rights or needs of the adopted person! Each point is concerned with the adoptive parent or birthparent. Point two goes on to state that "with the destruction of the traditional privacy of relinquishment, and the right of the adopted 'children' to the identities of their biological parents, relinquishing parents will be less likely to cope with the experience of birth and relinquishment. Lacking the security that they could put behind them this experience, social adjustment problems can be expected and the hope of any stable future family life will readily diminish." On behalf of thousands of birthparents - SECRECY never helped us to cope! In fact, just the opposite occurred. Because we were forced to suppress our true feelings, we attempted to deny reality and therefore our guilt and self-hatred about the surrender haunted us for years.

The article then goes on to say that "The rights accorded to relinquishing parents and adoptive children as adults under this Model Act would certainly be destructive to the emotional bonding process between the adopted "child" and the adoptive parents. The elevated levels of anxiety that adoptive parents would experience, could in many cases cause serious interference and severely threaten a normal and healthy relationship between parent and child."

Again and again, it cannot be emphasized enough - open records would in no way destroy the bonding that takes place between the adoptive parents and the child. If bonding has not taken place in 18 to 20 years of parenting, it never will!

This article, written by a Christian organization, does nothing but instill fear. They need to grasp the full meaning of the scripture verse "perfect (agape) love casts out fear."

Did pressure from agencies like the one above and the one that follows effect the deletion of the Open Records Section of the Model Adoption Act? I would suspect so.

Walter Deighan of La Jolla, California, sent me a copy of the following letter which he had written to CBS for consideration on their "60 Minutes" show. It describes his own experience as an adoptive parent with what he considers inhumane agency practices. I agree.

"Early in 1967 my wife and I, who were then residents of New York City, registered with a well-known adoption service. In August of 1968 we were invited by the agency to consider an infant, female child for adoption. Upon being told that the infant had been adjudged healthy by the agency doctor, and that the natural parents were two healthy teenagers, we accepted the baby with the greatest of pleasure and no reservations whatsoever.

In September of 1979, shortly after the child's eleventh birthday, she began to develop persistent head and neck pains which her pediatrician was at a loss to explain. To make an unhappy story a short one, the problem turned out to be a malignant brain tumor, and she died on April 7, 1980, exactly six months after being admitted to the hospital.

Around December of 1979, or January of 1980, it occurred to me that I should inform the agency what had happened. I thought this way for two reasons: 1) I assumed, naively perhaps, that they would want to communicate with the natural parents so that they might obtain medical assistance on the theory that this cancer might run in someone's family and early testing might make a difference; and 2) I assumed that the adoption agency would like to know about this situation merely on general priciples. I recalled clearly that the agency was very insistent on maintaining current records of location, place of employment, etc. in regard to the adoptive parents (would this also be their policy with the natural parents?) even after the adoption had been legalized by a judge. I recalled being somewhat surprised, even annoyed, that they continued to insist on knowing "what's happening" long after it appeared to me that it was any of their business.

Therefore, you may be able to understand my surprise, and subsequent anger and suspicion, when it turned out that the agency had a pronounced and complete *disinterest* in my situation. At the time I telephoned them, I asked to speak to the person in charge of adoptive services, whom we had met in 1967 and 1968, and had corresponded with subsequently. However, she was ill that day so I spoke to her assistant. As soon as I had given the gist of what I was calling about, she interjected the comment, "We didn't know anything about that." She listened to the rest of what I had to say with a kind of bored tolerance, which prompted me to ask her if she wouldn't want to communicate this information with the natural parents. She said that, "Oh, they *might* put a memo in the file *in case the woman ever wanted to put out another baby for adoption!"* Feeling strangely disappointed with this telephone conversation, I asked her to convey my story to the Director when the latter returned to the office, and I also left my current address and telephone number. Again, naively perhaps, the *least* I expected was some sort of pro formal letter of regret asking me to keep them informed of medical developments. What I heard from this "adoption service" was *absolutely nothing.*

Following my daughter's death in April of 1980, I began to develop strong feelings about the agency's indifference and callousness. I even wondered (and still do) if they had the decency to tell the natural mother that the child she had given up for adoption had died. It occurred to me that, if they attempted to communicate with the natural mother, they might in the process, learn something they would just as soon not know - such as the possibility that the natural mother, herself, had died of this disease, or, if she be unaffected, some other relative. To further fuel my anger and suspicion, I saw a television story concerning a grown man in Florida who had some form of cancer. This man had children of his own, and since he was adopted, he had some medical urgency to get in touch with his natural mother; since his natural mother's medical situation had some bearing on the man's or his children's prospects. As I recall, this man was getting the stonewall treatment both from adoption agencies and from judges - even though he appeared to have a perfectly valid claim for information.

I wondered if the same fate would befall me if I asserted, what I consider *my basic right to know what information,* if any, the agency had about the medical history of the natural parents before or *after* the adoption; and what standards they apply in checking the health backgrounds of persons who give up infants for adoption.

In November of 1980 I talked about this situation with my attorney here in San Diego, and he referred me to a New York City lawyer. The latter attempted to communicate with this adoption service by letter and by telephone and received no response.

The New York attorney told me that, for a substantial retainer, he will pursue the possibility of a fraud claim; but he feels that it would be quite difficult to get the agency to provide information without a judge's order, which order might be difficult or impossible to obtain. He also points out that there is no way of knowing, as opposed to suspecting, whether the agency has now, or has ever had, medical records and other possible information which might justify my concerns. Since there appears to be a six year statute of limitations in New York State for fraud claims, I don't have to make up my mind right away; but I can't understand why a person in my position has to face such tremendous potential expense in order to obtain something which I consider a basic human right. Evidently agencies have carte blanche to practice inhumanity par excellence!"

Mr. Deighan then added a note that his daughter's birth name was Cynthia Johnson and she was born August 6, 1968 in Lenox Hill Hospital in New York City.

I personally contacted the agency to discuss Mr. Deighan's matter with them and was told that it is not their policy to get back in touch with the birthparents no matter what the circumstances! The above is just one small example of the thousands concerning agency ineptness in providing important data to those directly involved in the adoption process. There are many other situations just as serious where agencies refuse to cooperate.

For instance, a dear birthmother friend from Michigan lost both her legs about four years ago. She had surrendered a child to adoption in 1967. In the last four years, she has attempted on various occasions to have her medical information relayed to the adoptive parents and/or their physician. The agency recently said they would pass the information along when they receive *three* separate letters in detail explaining Debbie's illness. The doctors do not even know what caused her problem! They do know that it's vascular in nature. Now the agency wants to be sure that the illness is hereditary before they agree to pass the information on. Since the doctors don't know what caused the problem in the first place, they have no way of knowing whether it's hereditary. But couldn't the agency contact the adoptive parents and/or their physician and make them aware that there may be a problem? Is that too much to ask?

Debbie's daughter was born March 16, 1967 in Providence Hospital in Detroit, Michigan. Maybe someone will be kind enough to pass this information along as preventive medicine!

A Matter of Control

Agencies, in general, do not support openness. While many claim to be more open, more often than not they are only giving lip service to those who contact them for help. But if and when "mutual consent" laws are passed, they will be the first ones to clamor for the "intermediary" role.

Jean Paton, mother of the adoption movement and a former social worker herself, has some strong views concerning this as stated in one of her newsletters:

"Social work loved the sealed record form of adoption and worked under it without the slightest protest for years and years. Now, when they see YOU (adoptees) breaking the chains which held you away from your roots, they seek to get in the midst of you and control your actions and mediate a reunion. When social workers do not believe in reunion, and many of them don't, they will destroy the possibility of one. If social work believed in reunion, they could begin at once, without any change in the laws. They would announce publicly that they are setting up Bureaus of Reconciliation in their offices, and be open and warm toward those who come in. They could give this as much publicity as the sealed record was given. No agency is to be trusted that is not willing to do this publicly and thoroughly."

Though much has already been written and discussed about the open records controversy, we need to continue our uphill battle until records are open in every state of our union - freeing those who are bound by it. More and more adoptive parents are beginning to recognize how unfairly they, too, have been treated by the agencies and are joining the rest of us dedicated to openness and honesty. It is for this cause that we are joined together. It is for this reason that we devote our time, our money, and our efforts. We will continue to fight for the right to our own records and for the right to make our own decision about contact.

The following questions are those most often asked by opponents of open records. While these questions have been answered throughout the book, it is only by repetitiveness that we seem able to grasp basic truths.

> 1) *Wouldn't open records disrupt the adoptive relationship and make it no more than long term foster care?*

Every form of parenting is "foster care" because all children grow up, hopefully to become independent, self-supporting individuals who establish supportive, loving bonds with many other people. This is imperative in our mobil society. If eighteen to twenty years of uninterrupted parenting doesn't result in full loyalty to that title, then that fact has nothing to do with adoption.

Parenting is a process, not a birth certificate. It creates over a period of time, an emotional bond that may or may not be associated with genetic ties. This phenomenon is happening in escalating numbers as millions of children are establishing parent bonds with more than one father and/or mother.

Adoptive Parents for Open Records is an organization of parents who support their adoptees in search and rejoice in lost identity links being found; who understand why they are not threatened by open records; who seek to change attitudes since the traditional concept of secrecy is outmoded. Their motto is "unselfish love reaches satisfaction in the happiness of our child."

2) Wouldn't open records increase abortions?

Research has shown that just the opposite is true. In talking to hundreds of teenagers, they claim they would have an abortion rather than give up a child to total strangers knowing they will never have the opportunity to meet. Some may have a great deal of difficulty understanding that, especially if you are against abortion. But I can also tell you from having "been there" that losing your child to adoption, and never knowing anything about that child, can be just as severe psychologically. Until we are willing to recognize and accept this fact and push for more openness in adoption, abortions will continue.

I do not support abortion; nor do I support closed adoption. Permanently closed adoption records make adoption as terminal as abortion. One cannot advocate maintaining the tie-of-life, while in the next breath nonchalantly suggest that once born, it is easy to sever the tie-of-life through permanently sealed records.

Dr. Sorosky, psychiatrist from the University of California and co-author of The Adoption Triangle, cited numerous cases in which unwed mothers stated they would place their child for adoption *only* if separation wasn't absolute.

3) Wouldn't open records mean that agencies would renege on their "promise" to the birthparents concerning confidentiality?

Concerned United Birthparents, Inc. a national birthparent organization, has repeatedly stated that birthparents never asked for or ever wanted the confidentiality structure that remains for their benefit. It was never a topic of discussion. Imposed confidentiality was the order of the day. Confidentiality was "guaranteed" because it was imposed upon the birthparent. It was a mere assumption that it was what the birthparent wanted.

Only in the United States and Canada is adoption set-up on such a 'grand pretense' whereby everyone is supposed to pretend that the birthparents are inconsequential figures.

Restoring Rights and Privileges

*Legislatures can act to take away an adoptee's right of access to his birth records, which they've done, but they cannot legislate away the perfectly natural need on the part of an adoptee to know the facts about his biological heritage.

Those adoptees who actively seek all information available about their origins feel this should be their right. Those who have not been adopted or cut off from their roots take this information for granted. We are on shaky ground if we believe it is legitimate to deny this information to those who do not now have their own automatic and easy access to it. Those adoptees who do not actively seek information beyond what they already have, would be free to continue without this knowledge even if there is the opportunity for access.

With respect to the relationship between adoptive parents and their offspring, therefore, what use can there be in legislation restricting access to one's own birth records?

Information about ancestry, cultural and ethnic history is normally transmitted through parents, grandparents, other extended family and friends, as a matter of course, as a child grows up. In the case of a person who has been adopted, he has a normal access to this information about his adoptive family, but does not have such access to information about his birth family. The adoptive family will have only a meager amount of this information to share with the child, as they usually have no first-hand contact with or knowledge of the birthparent and only a portion of the second-hand information shared with them by the adoption worker. It may have even been second-hand information to the adoption worker who may have received it verbally or from written records of another department of the agency. By the time these lifeless crumbs of one's life history reach the adopted child, they are at best third-hand or perhaps fourth-hand information. It is not difficult to understand the adopted person's dissatisfaction with this information as a source of enlightenment of their roots and origins.

To say that the number of adult adoptees who might wish access to such is insignificantly small is simply a timeworn effort to avoid discussing the issue on its merits. The conclusion implied in such a statement is that an adoptee who would like facts about his biological heritage and who might like to use these facts to find out more about his background is exhibiting aberrant behavior and is therefore not to be taken seriously. Such a conclusion could not be more erroneous.

The time, money and effort being spent in judicial and legislative opposition to birth records access by an adult adoptee, coupled with the resources expended by those searching, might be more wisely and more compassionately spent on outreach programs involving birthparents, adoptive parents and adoptees in an effort to promote more, not less, understanding surrounding this issue.

We would do well to heed the words of Judge Albert Tate of the Supreme Court of Louisiana in a dissenting opinion in a 1979 birth records access case: "nor can civil acts of human societies deprive a child of his ancestry and his membership by blood and descent in a family group--a family membership founded on unalterable laws of nature, which imparts to the individuals of the blood family a sense of the present self as forming an integral part of a greater whole of family continuing from the immeasurable past through the individual into the immeasurable future."

It is recognized that the present statutes stem from a three-fold interest:
- the best interest of the adoptee in establishing a relationship with his legal family;
- the interests of the adoptive parents in establishing a parent-child relationship;
- and the interest of the birthparents in availing themselves of the institution of adoption.

A careful analysis of each of these interests will demonstrate that the restoration to adult adoptees of their right to access and to receive information will not interfere with any of these interests.

1. *The Best Interests of the Adoptee*
    a. Legal Considerations - The adoptee merely asks that he be placed on an equal footing with other citizens with respect to the birth certificate. At the present time the adult adoptee is discriminated against inasmuch as direct access to his birth certificate is withheld for reasons beyond his control - the nature of his/her birth. Usually, the only recourse open to the adult adoptee is to petition the court. In practice, court orders of this nature are rarely granted on simple petition since courts will not interfere with legislatively established reasons for record sealing.

    This procedure of sealing the birth records permanently fails to recognize that the adopted child becomes an adult citizen at the age of majority. As an adopted adult he or she may enter into legal contracts, marry, hold, inherit, and devise property, etc. Although an adoptee who reaches the age of majority is considered an adult in all of these transactions, he or she remains the protected child adoptee and is denied access to vital personal records, despite the fact that the rationale for denial of equal protection by sealing records disappears when the protected child becomes an adult.

    The State of Kansas, which has never closed their records, has gone on record to say that "the advantages of a law that permits access to the original birth certificate by an adoptee of legal age significantly outweigh the disadvantages. We have had this provision in the statutes since 1943 and during that period of time there has apparently not been any noticeable effect upon the rates of adoption or abortion that could be attributed to the availability of the original birth record to the adopted person."

b. Medical Reasons - The American Academy of Pediatrics has warned, "Failure to provide and interpret significant medical information to prospective adoptive parents puts both child and parents at a great disadvantage." Though the unsealing of a birth certificate and subsequent revealing of other medical information at the age of majority cannot automatically produce a medical history from the birth family, the original certificate does give the adult adoptee the name of the delivering physician (usually omitted on amended certificates) and the names of the birthparents. In some cases the withholding of this information may be life-threatening not only to the adult adoptee but also to the adoptee's children. It is important that the adoptee's physician have a medical history in order to begin treatment against a particular disease. The medical history may also enable the physician to diagnose a disease that had previously been unrecognized. This history may also give the physician vital information about the adoptee's future health. Such information is routinely asked of patients by their doctors. But an adoptee usually cannot answer such a common question as, "Any history of heart attacks in your family?"

The National Foundation of the March of Dimes reports that some 943 dominantly inherited disorders and 783 recessively inherited disorders have been catalogued. Likewise, the National Institute of Child Health and Human Development reports that nearly 2,000 genetic defects have been found. It is important to note that some of these diesases and disorders do not manifest themselves at birth, but late in life.

Early knowledge of a genetic predisposition to a particular disease may permit the physician of the adoptee or his children to begin treatment either to avoid or mitigate the effects of the disease. An adult adoptee is denied this simple information. Only when a disease has been identified and often irrevocably advanced, does an adult adoptee have a chance to convince a court to break the legislative mandate which sealed the birth records.

c. Psychological Reasons - Recently, racial and ethnic groups have discovered the fundamental importance of their roots in understanding their identity and have taken steps to develop their histories and discover their cultural, social, and biological past. The development of a personal identity is essential to a healthy productive life. The secrecy surrounding the adoptee's preadoptive life not only leaves him with a frustrating gap in his self-image, but frequently suggests to him that there is something unacceptable about him or his origins. His ability to form a complete personal identity is frustrated by the very governmental action intended to help him.

Psychiatrist-Author Robert Jay Lifton notes (in the Foreword to Politics of Adoption, by M. K. Benet, 1976) that this system of secrecy is seen as a 'dirty little secret' about the adoptee's origins. The whole system is structured to make the adoptee feel that he should not think about his origins and that he should suppress his desire to know. But in trying to do so, he tries to suppress the unsuppressable. His psychological makeup - like nature in general - abhors a vacuum and the void is filled in by fantasies. The fantasies may be of various types, but it is better for the adoptee to deal with the truth of his origins - no matter how distasteful or negative this information may be in the eyes of others - than to attempt to deal with fantasies for his entire life. This fact is seldom recognized by non-adoptees and it is this non-recognition which has led to many abuses in the present system whereby well-meaning adoption workers have been known to withhold or distort what they felt was destructive information when it is sought by adoptive parents or adoptees. At the very least, adoption workers are very uncomfortable in handling such information. It is best that no one be put in the role of deciding just what particular piece of information the adoptee is or is not entitled to.

2. *The Adoptive Parents*

With respect to the interests of the government in insuring the establishment of a stable parent-child relationship between the adoptee and the adoptive parents, there is no evidence that making original birth records available to adult adoptees will frustrate this purpose. The person who has reared the child and has had daily contact with him becomes his "psychological parent". In other words, the adoptee develops an emotional attachment to the adoptive parents, as a result of their day-to-day attention to his physical care, nourishment, comfort, affection and stimulation, which is lacking for an absent birthparent. Even those adult adoptees who may contact birthparents recognize their adoptive family's unique personality and consider their adoptive parents their true parents.

The adoptee's inquisitiveness about his natural origins is very often misinterpreted as an attempt to find "another set of parents." An adoptee's need for information about his natural origins have to do with his quest for identity, not a search for other parents. Thus, such information about his natural origins merely complements the adoptee's personality; it does not replace any relationship which has already been established. Furthermore, an adoptee's need to know about his natural origins has nothing to do with gratitude or lack of gratitude towards his adoptive parents. This need also exists no matter how nurturing the adoptive family has been.

It stretches the imagination to conceive of a valid argument that would say that an adoptive parent should have a right protected in the law that denies the person who was raised in his or her family the right to know his origins. Adult adoptees have affirmed and reaffirmed the reality that knowledge of and contact with their birthparents does not supersede, set aside, or change the fundamental nature of their relationship with their adoptive parents. It has been our experience with adult adoptees, that the adoptive parent who is able to support and give his blessing to his adopted "child's" right and need to know his birthparents finds that his own relationship with the "child" enriched and enhanced. The adoptive parent who feels the need to deny his "child" this right contributes to the alienation of his "child" from himself. This hardly seems to be in the real interests of either party.

Further, the view has been expressed that prospective adoptive parents would decline to adopt if they thought that adoptees would ultimately have access to information about their birthparents. First, as noted above, the unsealing of the birth certificate would not constitute an intrusion into the family relationship at a time when the relationship was developing. Second, in those states where the adult adoptee has access to his birth certificate and in those foreign countries where access to various records is provided, the opening of records has not been shown to inhibit the adoption of children. In addition, there are few agencies today in the United States which promise prospective parents that records will remain unsealed.

3. *The Birthparents*

The oft-heard argument for keeping the records sealed is that the natural mother has a right to privacy, thus she does not want her life disrupted by a child she has given up and forgotten. Interestingly enough, this argument is usually unsupported by any data whatsoever and is frequently an emotional reaction of people who have not actually experienced the circumstances of pregnancy, motherhood, and separation.

Since some birthmothers do not want the immediate world to know of the birth, she may be reluctant to testify publicly or even discuss the matter with strangers. However, this reluctance to go public should not be misunderstood and applied narrowly to affect the adult adoptee. To say that a birthmother, who once gave up a child for adoption does not want the public to know, is not to say that she wishes to maintain secrecy or that she even has a right of total privacy vis-a-vis her birthchild.

What the opponents of open records forget is that between the birthmother and her child, there is never a right of privacy with respect to the incidence of birth. The woman by her signature, often under duress and in a difficult time, cannot forget that she has given birth to a human being. There is no right of privacy between the child and its mother as to the fact of birth, for every human is born of a woman and no sealing of records, no cloak of secrecy, no act in the name of privacy can wash away that fact.

They have also argued that the continued anonymity of the birthparents is necessary to maintain the integrity of the adoption process because anonymity is the parents' major consideration in deciding to let their child out for adoption. Disclosure, it is argued, might have an inhibitory effect on adoptions. It is claimed that the young pregnant woman may choose to have an abortion, or if it is too late for that, to rear the child herself rather than face the possibility of meeting him 18 or 21 years later. There is little doubt that many persons at the time they relinquish a child even consider the protection they receive through the policy of secrecy. It is not a factor in the decision to relinquish. In fact, *it is the finality of the decision under the present law which makes birthmothers hesitate about relinquishing the child; the thought they will never know anything about the welfare of this child is a terrifying one.*

*Excerpts from a presentation by Les Waguespack to the Louisiana legislature, February, 1981.

What About Open Adoption?

It's obvious that we need to begin to change adoption practices. What about open adoption? What is it? Open adoption is a form of adoption during which adoptive parents and birthparents have varying degrees of contact during which respective identities may or may not be known to the consenting parties. This adoption is less of an amputation for the birthparent and enables the adoptive parents to form a *stable* parent-child relationship free from fear, anxiety, secrecy and denial.

Gloria Veillon of the Adoptees Birthright Committee of Lafayette, Louisiana, suggests that, before the institution of adoption is relatively non-existant, those who previously opposed any change open their hearts and minds to at least explore open adoption. She says that adult adoptees who are searching for their birthparents are being blamed for the ever-increasing abortion rate. This seems to be fostered by some pro-life groups. If pro-life groups are *truly* concerned with the preservation of life, then she suggests they begin to work with us in promoting open adoption. I add my amen to that. I believe that only when open adoptions become the law of the land, will abortions begin to diminish.

On December 9, 1981, a public hearing on an open records bill was held in Trenton, New Jersey. Harold Cassidy an attorney from north Jersey stated that he was there, not as a lawyer, but as a witness to human suffering. "In this forum, it is greatly less important what is presently the law, than understanding what we ought to make it for the future. The need for change in the law that we perceive is based on reality.

The birthmother makes the sacrifice that we cannot even conceive of making - she surrenders her child out of total dedication to the welfare of the child, because she is led to believe that that is the best course. We must accept the responsibility for this act because as a society, we are the ones who have urged the surrender. Our hypocrisy is in our punishment of the young mother. We condemn her to a lifetime of suffering. The truth is that in her time of need, if we directed our energy and resources in giving her support, rather than urging surrender, there would be much less need for adoption in the first instance.

I have seen the pain of the mother in South Carolina who tearfully calls me begging for help. She had surrendered her child two years earlier. Ten days after she had signed a piece of paper, she asked for the return of the baby. Four days after she was refused, she sought court intervention, but she will never see her child again.

What is it about this peice of paper that makes it so impenetrable, so above all present legal principles that apply to other documents? Such a system must be held suspect. As a society, we must examine our conscience. We must be bold enough to inquire whether we are supplying homes for children who need them, or whether we are really only supplying children to feed an adoption system."

At the same hearing Dr. Herbert Wieder, a psychoanalyst and psychiatrist spoke as a mental health advocate after studying and researching the psychological lives of adopted people, as well as adoptive parents and birthparents. His main conclusion was that the closed secret records have had a deleterious psychological effect on each member of the triangle.

Concerning the birthmother, he said, "The

birthmother's sense of guilt and shame, compounded by an overt condemnation by society, has kept them in a self-isolate prison of silence." His relevant findings were: 1) Relinquishment in the physical sense took place, but in the psychological sense, never did; 2) Immediate consequences of remorse to the physical surrender turned into a long-term pathological mourning. The psychological preparedness for mothering occasioned by the months of pregnancy was left unfulfilled. A feeling that the baby was dead, but not dead, was real, but not real, which would have been modified by even discussions about the baby were to remain untouched; 3) The baby remained a reality, however, in the mind of the mother, and many women grew the child in their minds. This represents a very severe compromise with reality. Lack of realistic information fuel the fires of fantasy as the supplier of information; 4) Self-condemnation for their surrender became chronic self-degradation and guilt associated with fantasies of the life they imagined the child was living. The lost child theme became a preoccupation. Sometimes this preoccupation led to the exclusion of other later reality-oriented relationships, and all their interests and emotions centered on their fears for the lost child; 5) The young person who relinquished, grew up sadder and wiser. Most knew they could not and would not want to recapture the past. They only want to ease what any parent might feel compelled to – their anxieties about the child, their fears and their guilts."

Both of these gentlemen see the need for open adoption right from the start. More and more people in the helping professions are beginning to recognize that adoptees have to not only know about, but also remain connected with their historical and genetic past in significant ways throughout their lives.

A Chinese proverb says, "A man falls back on legalities when he has no moral grounds on which to stand." The present adoption system cannot be defended on moral grounds because it is unfair and unjust; therefore we try to justify it on legal grounds. Adoption as we know it today was a legal invention of the 40's - it was a misguided attempt to both imitate nature on the one hand and help those who had gone "astray" on the other hand. We now know that it created many more problems than it ever hoped to solve. Therefore, open adoption must become the order of the day.

But is open adoption really possible and feasible? Can it work? According to Barbara Tremitiere, Director of Adoption Services for Tressler-Luthern Services of York, Pennsylvania, "adoption is shared parenthood. Biologically and genetically, we did not give our children life. Studies have shown, over the years, that to share parenthood does not have to mean that someone "loses" and someone "wins". To the contrary, studies show that adoptive families who helped their children find and incorporate past history into their lives actually seem to end up with a closer relationship to the adoptive family that raised them."

She goes on to say that "Many families even feel comfortable participating in open adoption relationships while their children are growing up. Recognizing the reality of "shared parenthood" and its implication. . .going beyond the jealousy that comes from claiming "ownership" of a child we didn't produce. . .helps us come to grips with the realities and potentials of many different forms of open adoptions. I believe we will find more of these open relationships occurring in the future as we come to grips with the fact that to share a child's life may well be a major factor in enhancing the quality of the relationship the parents have and maintain with that child."

Barbara is also an adoptive mother. She said that when they first adopted their son, and were about to have him baptized, someone asked if they were standing in for his parents! At that time they emphatically said, "No, we are his parents". She said that were she to face that person today, she would answer quite differently. "Yes, we are standing in for the parents who gave him birth. For a variety of reasons, they could not raise him, so we are standing in to do that job".

Beyond the Shadow of Secrecy

A national ad hoc committee was recently established to re-evaluate adoptive placement philosophy. Community, Family & Children Services of Traverse City, Michigan, hosted the first national conference on Open Placement Adoption in April, 1982. The committee, agency, and participants are to be commended for taking this giant step toward humanizing the adoption process. Reuben Pannor, Director of Community Services at Vista Del Mar Child-Care Service in Los Angeles, California, and co-author of The Adoption Triangle, spoke about The Case for Open Adoptions as Standard Practice. Following his most informative talk, the conference participants "adopted" and endorsed a position paper which states:

> Open adoption is an acknowledgement of the lifetime relationship among adoptees, birth families and adoptive families in which legal custody is transferred. It includes, but is not limited to, the mutual exchange of full identities prior to finalization of adoption, the right to continuing contact and knowledge of the whereabouts and welfare of all parties and offers an appreciation of the unique contribution of those involved.
>
> It is the consensus of the conference participants that the secrecy, and anonymity, and

mystique that has surrounded the traditional adoption of the past has left behind numerous psychological problems for adoptees, birth families and adoptive families. This practice must be replaced by a form of adoption that practices openness and honesty and thereby permits a healthier and psychologically sounder adoption practice.

It is our conviction that open adoption must be the prevailing practice in all independent and agency adoptions."

Two agencies that are practicing some form of open adoption are Catholic Social Services of Green Bay, Wisconsin, and Luthern Social Services of San Antonio, Texas. As part of the adoption process at Luthern Social Services, the birthparent is involved in the selection of the adoptive parents for her child. Social histories about the prospective adoptive parents reflect education, lifestyle, background, interests, talents, etc. The birthparent privately reviews the background information about these families and selects the family with which she feels most comfortable raising her child. In this way, the birthparents participate in the plan for their child, actively assuming responsibility in the decision-making process. This further gives reassurance regarding their decision.

The birthparent may then correspond with the adoptive parents. They are encouraged to include pictures of themselves and their families. All this is done to dispel fantasies and fears of the unknown. Being treated in a humane and caring manner makes the birthparent feel worthwhile and respected. The openness of the adoption process has made it possible for birthparents to come to grip more easily with their decision and go on with their lives.

Adoptive parents are also a central focus since they come to the agency with one main focus: they want a child. In order to move from that stage to one encompassing an understanding and sensitivity to adoption issues, the agency has intensive day long seminars that focus on issues such as infertility, how to tell the child he's adopted, feelings towards birthmothers, etc. A panel of birthmothers participate in this seminar. This helps all parties to become sensitized to one another and dispels any fantasies they may have about the kind of people who are involved with adoption. Adoptive parents are also given options which include correspondence, sending pictures of their child to the birthmother, etc.

The newest dimension of their program is the option of a face to face meeting between the birthparent(s) and the adoptive parents of her (their) child. This meeting only occurs when both parties desire to exercise this option. The rationale for this is that through direct contact *all* fantasies are dispelled and the adoptive family will obtain valuable first-hand information to share with their child through the years. This option benefits all three parties in the adoption triangle.

The entire adoption program at Luthern Social Service of Texas revolves around the philosophy that all parties involved must be served through the adoption process. Through education and counseling, adoptive parents become comfortable with their role and the issues they will confront. This has ramifications for better parenting, not just when they first become parents to an infant and his needs at the time, but also when their child goes through all the developmental stages and reaches adulthood with corresponding needs.

Birthparents are also better able to proceed with their lives having had support and options before and after the adoption has occurred. The central person, the adoptee, in whose 'best interest' the adoption plan was made, reaps the benefits of this openness, education, and sharing in which his adoptive and birthparents participated.

In this way, it can be said that adoption practices of this kind encompasses preventive mental health. Their literature advocates it and practice confirms it.

Legislation recently introduced in Massachusetts would make openness impossible. A bill entitled "An Act Protecting the Integrity of an Adopting Family and Safeguarding the Family in its Right to Privacy and Confidentiality" would prohibit any agency from forwarding letters or information between birth and adoptive families, releasing identifying information to any party, or facilitating reunions between consenting people. It would mandate that all adoptions be closed adoptions regardless of whether the parties involved wanted it that way. Any agency violating the provisions of this Act would be subject to revocation of its license for up to five years. This legislation was suggested by an adoptive parents' group and supported by Goliath (NCFA).

Need I comment on its absurdity? When adoptive parents in greater numbers receive the kind of counseling and input provided by an agency like Luthern Social Services of San Antonio, then the threatened feelings that caused the proposal of this bill will be greatly diminished.

Ambiguities in the Law

A series of articles dealing with various aspects of adoption was recently published by one of the Surrogates' Offices in New Jersey. In quoting from an article entitled "Adopted Children - A Search for Identity", it explains how to facilitate a reunion under New Jersey State Law.

"The first is by going directly to the agency which handled the adoption. If an adopted child, over 18 years of age, or natural parent presents a request for a reunion, the adoption agency has a duty to do their best to find the child or natural parent and present them with the option. However, if the child or parent rejects the reunion, the adoption agency can not divulge either the name or address of either party to the other. The next step for the person desiring the reunion would be to bring an action before the Superior Court Probate Section, requesting that he/she be given the name and address of the adopted child or natural parent, whichever the case may be.

The Court must base its decision on whether or not it would be in the best interest of the "child" to be reunited with his/her parent. Generally, if the child is asking for the information, and if *expert witnesses* like a doctor or psychologist, testify that a reunion would be in the adoptees' best interest, the Courts are increasingly granting the request and the child is presented with the name and address of the natural parent.

In cases where the natural parent is requesting that the Court release information on the child and the child has already denied the request made through the adoption agency, there is usually little chance for the parent to win the case.

Why?? Because the overriding principle remains whether or not a reunion would be in the best interest of the child and *the adoptees' personal wishes are the strongest factor in the Court's decision as to what is in the child's best interest.*"

Read those last few paragraphs again. Do you note what I do? When it comes to refusing the birthparent, the adoptees' personal wishes are the strongest factor in the Court's decision as to what is in the child's best interest! That's as it should be. But when the adoptee wants to have a reunion with the birthparents, they need *expert witnesses* and then the Court will decide if it's in "the child's" best interest! Please remember that "the child" may be 50 years old!!

In another article entitled "Subsidized Adoptions" it states that "if you need financial help, you may be eligible for a flat monthly fee to be used in meeting the costs of raising the child." It is not specified what makes one eligible for this flat fee. At first I thought it was specifically for those who were adopting handicapped or other special needs, but as I read on it discussed a second type of subsidized adoption called the "special service subsidy" which is granted to cover legal fees, medical costs related to a medical condition or special needs such as speech, physical therapy or special training. If you qualify for the first type of maintenance subsidy, you may receive up to 80 percent of what it would cost the State to care for the child if the child were placed in a foster home. But it doesn't mention what the qualifications are to receive this type of subsidy.

The reason most children are placed for adoption is because the mother cannot financially manage. When she does decide to keep her baby and is subsidized (via state aid), we criticize and belittle her; yet we applaud subsidized adoption for "other" parents. Children are placed in foster care often for the same reason. When are we going to begin to provide practical services that will enable the natural family to remain together?

Social workers have told me that natural parents whose children are in the foster system don't really care about them; that they just want free baby-sitters, but don't want the responsibility. I realize that there may be a small minority for which that kind of statement holds true. However, the mother who does not care about her child or want that child with her are few and far between. Let's look at the other side of the coin and see how, in some instances, subtle pressure was applied to the unwed and single mother that caused the child to be placed in foster care in the first place.

It was often suggested that she place her child in foster care so she could "get her act together." In the meantime, she was neither encouraged nor permitted to visit because "it's too disruptive for the child," "the child needs to bond with the foster parent," etc. In most cases, she was not even told where the child had been placed. If she was permitted visitation, the child was placed far away - making it difficult or impossible to get there. Six months later the same "helpful" social worker appears in court with 'substantial evidence' showing that the parent never bothered or attempted to visit the child (abandonment they call it) and suddenly her rights are involuntarily surrendered. Since she is young and/or poor, she cannot retain a lawyer and so it's her word against the "professional" social worker. Does this happen? Is it happening? You bet your life it is.

The agencies in the past have perpetuated the foster care system. Why? Because it was financially in their "best interest" to do so. They received subsidy funds for each child placed and kept in foster care. Foster care was big business. Now that funds are being cut, "permanent planning" has become the key word, and "freeing" them for adoption.

Many of these children have been in foster care from the time they were born. I wonder how many of the birthparents are aware that their children, surrendered at birth, are stuck in the foster care system. I wonder how many agencies have even bothered to contact them to see if they are in a position to have their child with them.

One birthmother, who had surrendered her child at birth, found 12 years later that her son had never been adopted - nor had she been informed! Another birthmother found her 12 year old in an institution. He had been placed there at the age of six following the death of his adoptive mother. His adoptive father had remarried and the new wife did not want the responsibility of raising "someone else's child". This birthmother has since adopted her own child.

Most agree that the entire social work field needs to be reformed. But it's unfortunate that those working within the system are so reluctant to make those changes. The above cited cases are but a few of thousands. Changing social prejudices is not an easy task, especially when it involves the "unpardonable" sin - being pregnant out-of-wedlock. Sometimes the people who have the most difficulty coping with it are those who are going through the experience - as the following story illustrates.

A 39 year old woman recently contacted me for help. She had been married for fourteen years and had adopted a child. She was told by a dozen doctors that she would never conceive her own child. Three years ago she and her husband divorced. She became involved with someone she cared for and eventually became pregnant. What should she do?

As we continued to talk, I noticed something interesting begin to develop in the conversation. She began to express the same kind of scared, frightened, insecure feelings I had had 27 years ago. It's called the "unwed mother syndrome". "What will people say? Will my child be accepted? Am I a terrible person?" And so on. She had even left her home in Florida and traveled north to stay with her brother. That way she could give up her child, return to her job, the neighbors wouldn't know, and her sanctity would be intact! Ah, what tangled webs we weave, when first we practice to deceive!

Does the repertoire sound familiar? After all, how would she handle the stigma of returning home with a child? (I suggested that she tell everyone she adopted him; not only would they readily accept that explanation, but they'd think she was a wonderful person for doing so!) Now I know that what I just said is going to make some people very angry, but think about it. Isn't it true? Society lauds the parent who adopts, but condemns the *same* person who chooses to keep their "out-of-wedlock" child. Why?

Marianne had visited several adoption agencies prior to contacting me. She said it did not take her long to realize that she was carrying a valuable product and one which the agency was interested in procuring. She also said that she could understand how easy it would be for a young person to yield to their pressure, subtle as it was.

We discussed the pros and cons of keeping her child and she decided that the pros far outweighed the cons. This had been the desire of her heart for so many years, as well as an answer to her many prayers - untimely, yes - unwanted, no. Mother and child are together - as God intended.

A System Built on Deceit Will Crumble

Jo Anne Swanson, author of the following article, joins me in asking our fellow-Christians - "Isn't it about time we Christians took a long, thorough, compassionate look at what we've done to one another through the closed records system of adoption?"

God reminds us throughout His Word that His Way is one of absolute, uncompromising TRUTH. Sometimes He refers to it as "Light" as in the scripture "God is Light, and in Him is no darkness at all." I John 1:5.

How very distressed He must be with the devious system mankind has devised to "legitimize" its illegitimate children! As if a doctored-up birth certificate could change THE PERSON who was known by Him even while he was yet in his mother's womb! God's Plan of Salvation for us has NOTHING to do with legal documents, aristocratic blood (or lack of it) or any other act of man, intentional or unintentional.

It seems significant to me that one of the ways adoptees have described their frustration with the closed records system is that, as one adoptee put it, "I'm forced to feel my way around in total darkness, while some total stranger in a well-lighted room has access to all the files which contain the very truths I'm seeking!"

Jesus said, "I am the Way, the Truth and the Life. No

man comes to the Father, but by me." I know I speak for thousands of others when I say that it is impossible to justify the sealed records system when measured against the TRUTH of Jesus Christ! It seems as though every institution of adoption is fraught with lies of one kind or another.

Perhaps the most resented lie of all is the falsified certificate of birth. The amended birth certificate is, pure and simple, a legal lie!

By going back to the beginning of the adoption process we can see that lies were woven into the fabric of most adoptions. In many cases the birthparents had plans to marry, or were willing to marry and make a home for their child. Instead, the couple was pitted against one another by well-meaning parents - telling him to deny he was the father and telling her that he had skipped out on her. Then she was whisked away to a maternity home. To family and friends, of course, she was "away at camp" or "visiting Aunt Sadie".

Lie upon lie - but just the beginning! At the maternity home, lies were the order of the day. The inmates were given pseudonyms to use during their stay to protect them against future contacts by other inmates. Phone calls to an inmate by friends who were not approved in advance met with further lies. "We have no one here by that name."

As the time neared for each inmate's baby to be born, she was coached concerning how to live the lie that she had not given birth to a baby out of wedlock. "Don't tell the man you marry. He doesn't have to know."

HOW MANY UNWED MOTHERS HAVE LIVED IN CONSTANT, UNRELENTING FEAR AND CRUSHING GUILT BECAUSE OF THAT ADVICE?

Next she is told that she will "forget" and "go on with her life" and eventually the pain will go away. Over 90% of the women who have surrendered a child to adoption know that's one of the biggest lies of all.

After assuring her that her child will be far better off raised by two parents, and that she can't possibly give her child what it needs, she lets her concern for her child's well-being take precedent over her own motherly instincts. This may not be interpreted as a lie in and of itself, but you can't convince some adoptees and birthmothers of this!

Ask the adoptees whose adoptive parents ended up getting divorced and they were raised by a single parent anyway. Ask the birthmother from Texas who recently found her relinquished son in a juvenile detention home, the result of his father having been a child abuser and his mother a drug addict. Ask the woman adoptee about her alcoholic adoptive father and his carryings on with women, etc., etc.

"Now wait just a minute", you're saying! All adoptive parents are not drinkers, abusers, or terrible people. YOU'RE RIGHT, of course! After all, "natural" parents have done terrible things to their own children.

But I have to vigorously defend my point. When a birthmother is led to believe, by someone she trusts, that the child will be cared for better, and then that adoption turns out badly, for HER the entire adoption system is a pathetic lie! And for the adoptee who has fared badly in the game of "parent substitution", it is indeed seen as a cruel lie to be forced to live out his entire life with his identity arranged from behind a desk somewhere!

Next, the deceit is passed on to the adoptive parents to carry out. For the most part, it is up to them to decide whether or not they will tell their child of his being adopted. Most do, if for no other reason than out of fear lest the child learn the truth from someone else. And then comes the decision as to what to tell the child in regard to his birthmother not keeping him. As B. J. Lifton points out in her book "Twice Born" - any author knows that the way to dispense with unwanted characters in a story is to kill them off. Neat and tidy! Adoptees get together at search group meetings and laugh (on the outside) at their own fallibility when they were told that their dad died in "the war", when in fact there was no war at the time of their birth. Or that their parents died in a car accident on the way to the hospital; mother living just long enough to give birth. You can imagine the impact that the real truth has on the parent-child relationship sometime later when the child (now adult) searches for and finds his very-much alive birthparents and learn they were simply young, unwed lovers!

I have been working for several months with a precious woman adoptee who only recently learned of her adoptive status - she's in her mid-30's. As if that weren't bad enough, she also learned that she was the only one in her entire family who was "kept in the dark" about it - cousins, aunts, uncles - everybody else knew. The pain she struggles with from day to day is not so much the fact of her being adopted, but the deception of her parents all these years.

"...in Him is no darkness at all."

Let's not forget the deceptions carried on in many adoption agencies throughout the country in regard to inquiries made by adoptees and birthparents. It's common for all three sides of the adoption triangle to be pleading with an agency for release of information and for them each to be told that the others' anonymity must be "protected". Agencies feel perfectly free to speak on behalf of birthmothers, urging adoptees allow them the dignity of anonymity, when in fact the birthmother is searching feverishly from the other end!

Court clerks have lied outright to searchers, giving them false information that has added months - even years - to their searches. Birthmothers have been lied to by doctors, who said that their babies died, and then have been found years later by those supposedly-dead children! Adoptive parents have been lied to, assured that the "girl" who surrendered her baby did so willingly, when in truth she was misled into thinking the papers she was signing were for "temporary foster care." Birthfathers have been lied to, told that their babies were miscarried, throwing them off the track while the birthmothers are whisked off somewhere. Adoptees have been lied to - told that their birthmothers "didn't want them" while in truth their birthmothers cried, pleaded and begged to keep them!

Lies! Darkness of the blackest kind - yet all allowed under the existing adoption system.

I cannot believe that God meant for any of His children to fumble around in the darkness for their very own identities. His own Son, Jesus Christ, could trace His human ancestry directly back to Adam!

I also find it very difficult to believe that a loving God would form a baby in a mother's womb and then approve of a system which prevents that mother from ever seeing that child again. Do you remember Sarah's answer to her infertility problem? Actually this was the earliest known case of what we now call surrogate mothering. Sarah simply turned over her handmaid to her husband Abraham and he fathered Ishmael through Hagar. Now I don't for one minute recommend this particular method of parenting for our day, but the point must be made that in God's plan for this child, his birthmother, Hagar, was not excluded from Ishmael's life, but was retained as caregiver. This is the loving, caring God I believe in. If you just stop and think for one minute about our adoption system, how can the Christian faith justify our inhumane system of mother-replacement?

Moses' mother after lovingly weaving that tiny reed basket and setting her dear son afloat, was NOT kept in the dark about the child of her womb. The Lord saw to it that she was appointed as the child's nurse, and the child Moses retained his Hebrew heritage and purpose in spite of his Egyptian adoption.

No darkness at all.

(Reprint from Roots & Reunions, May, 1982)

If He Inquires
by Patricia Horn-O'Brien

Dear Social Worker:
This September, the solemn month
of summer's turn from light,
its ploughing under,
my son becomes 18.
But do not ask me to describe
some telling detail of his face,
if he wears a hat
or is among the young men I have watched
protest the wind bareheaded.
Although I am his mother
I only guess he is a dreamer
slouching toward a waiting city,
his long legs stretched
across the bus's aisle,
a magazine rolled in his pocket,
only guess his name.

But no matter.

If he calls on you, you will know him
by cross-referenced files
and print-out of his vital fact,
his first breath matched
precisely with a time and date
and name exchanged, on his behalf,
with the name I breathed
to join his bones,
to fill his veins.

But someone overlooked that blazing summer
of the ripening fruit,
its harvest offered to a god
that was not kind,

and marked the records "Closed"
against all sadness,
against the possibility of tears.

I was left to guess his eyes
among the fields
of countless autumn boys.

But no matter.

If he comes to you and asks where is my mother
from whose breast cruel fate has plucked me,
sweet momma who adored me,
who cannot sleep nor sing with open throat
for fear her baby is not well
or does not love her
of if he says where is that bitch
who tossed me over to a hungry never-mother
so she could keep her thighs wide over
a life of her own,
where's that slut who only sighed and dropped me
from her rented space
or if he pounds upon your desk,
insists it is his right to know the symbols
on his family crest,
(he envisions, at times, a unicorn,
at times a sword-crossed crown)
insists he will not meddle
with blood broken 18 years ago,
he simply needs to know
who he has been,
who he will be,

tell him, please, he will find me
these days of early darkness
waiting by my door
at the following address:

SECTION V

THE ADOPTION MOVEMENT
AND PROJECT AWARENESS

"The adoptee rights movement which began as a mere trickle will soon become a river whose powerful tide will sweep all opposition before it".

Warren Siegmond, Author

Brief Background of the Adoption Movement

In 1954, Jean Kittson Paton, an adoptee and social worker, wrote an article called The Adopted Break Silence and formed a group called Orphan Voyage. She first called her work the Life History Study Center. In her own words, "The one unifying concept in the sciences is life history, and so us. Then I found it confirmed in The Adopted Break Silence; the search being a theme which recurs throughout a life until it is ended with reunion." She has several pieces of literature available which can be ordered by writing Orphan Voyage, Cedaredge, Colorado 81413. Her most recent ones are entitled "My Mother - A Tale of Reconciliation" and "What Happened to Adoption?" Both articles are interesting and informative.

Jean was alone in her quest until 1971 when Florence Fisher wrote about her twenty year search. She began one of the largest national adoption activist organizations in the country known as ALMA - Adoptees Liberty Movement Association.

In the early to mid-70's other groups began springing up across the country. Some of those early groups included the Adoption Forum, Adoptees Identity Movement, Adoptees In Search, Always In Me, Operation Identity, Reunite, Search, Truth Seekers In Adoption and Yesterday's Children. Those groups primarily represented adoptees until

1976 when Lee Campbell founded Concerned United Birthparents - a support group for those who had surrendered children to adoption. CUB is now nationwide and has representatives and branches in many states.

In 1979 the local organizations met in Washington, D.C. for their first national conference and 'adopted' the name American Adoption Congress. The AAC became an official organization in 1981 and now represents hundreds of activist groups around the country.

In addition to the search and support groups, there are four national service organizations. They are the International Soundex Reunion Registry (ISRR), Post-Adoption Center for Education and Research (PACER), Triadoption Library, and Adoption Triangle Ministries (ATM).

ISRR is a free reunion registry enabling people to register their data in order to effect a match between parties. Emma May Vilardi, Founder and Registrar, in her recent annual report states that the registry was increased by 4,260 in the past 12 month period. It is the largest multi-project of its kind. In the same report were other interesting statistics. Among her registrants are 38 sets of twins who were reared together, 47 sets of twins that were separated by adoption and in search of their twin sibling, and 21 sets of twins that are being sought by their birthparents. To request a registry form, see appendix for address.

Triadoption Library is a multi-education center. In 1981 they responded to over 3,600 requests for assistance. Triadoption provides a referral service, a speakers bureau, reference material, search and support classes, etc. The Adoption Searchbook, one of their publications, is a great aid for those persons desiring to locate information and/or people.

The Post-Adoption Center for Education and Research is located at 860 Bryant St., Palo Alto, California 94301. PACER studies all aspects of search, reunion, genetics, as well as the emotional and psychological effects that adoption has had upon its members. PACER has become a great resource center, particularly to agencies considering changes in their policies.

Adoption Triangle Ministries is another multi-faceted organization. ATM provides speakers to church groups, private agencies, and pro-life organizations. Their publications have a spiritual emphasis related to adoption, as does their tape outreach. Informal rap sessions for all members of the triad are held periodically. For a packet of sample leaflets and material, send a self-addressed stamped envelope along with $2.00 to ATM, Box 156, Oaklyn, New Jersey 08107.

The foregoing service organizations serve the entire adoption movement as well as society in general. Feel free to call upon them.

A new support group that needs recognition is one called TRACN which stands for Transracial Adoptees Communication Network. The concept for this organization arose from the need to find and communicate with other people of color (Blacks, Asians, Latino, Chicanos, and Native Americans) who are adopted and searching for their racial and cultural identities, as well as their biological roots. The group adds yet another relatively unexplored dimension to the adoption triangle

When I first heard about TRACN, I recalled the case of a white birthmother who had subsequently married the black birthfather. When her daughter turned 18 she did a search for her, only to learn that she had never been told of her mixed origins. The information had been withheld. Since she was lightskinned, she passed for Italian and was never the wiser. The adoptive parents never dreamed that one day she would learn the truth.

Alma Goodard, originator of TRACN states "In searching for the pieces of ourselves, we need to include a complete picture in relation to the racial and cultural separation we have experienced through the adoption process. Let us explore these dimensions together." For more information, write her at 4726 S.E. Taylor Avenue, Portland, Oregon 97215.

A few other newly formed support groups are United Adoptees & Parents, 9303 Bullard, Clovis, California 93612; Central Coast Adoption Support, Box 1937, Santa Maria, California 93455; Parents & Adoptees Uplifted, Rt. 1, Box 71, Williams, Arizona 86046; The Lost Children, 312 8th Avenue, St. Albans, West Virginia 25177 and Reaching Out, Box 42749, Los Angeles, CA, which provides personal consultation and search help for a fee.

Independent Search Consultants and Adoption Consultants also provide search help and consultation for a fee. See appendix for addresses.

To be kept abreast of what is going on in the movement, it would be well for you to become a member of the American Adoption Congress. What is the AAC? It is a coalition of individuals and groups across North America who care about making adoption more open; it is an acknowledgement of the many people who, on their own or in groups, are working toward this goal in a variety of ways; it is a means of educating ourselves about adoption change and a channel through which we can educate the rest of the adoption community and the general public; it is an opportunity for groups, large and small, to learn from each other, and for individuals, whether in a group or not, to connect with the larger network.

You can join the AAC by sending your check of $20 to Heidi Taylor, AAC Treasurer, 573 Hollyburne Lane, Thousand Oaks, California 91360. You will receive a national newsletter and be kept informed of AAC activity within your region. Regional conferences are held usually in the fall and the national conference is held in the spring. The 1982 national conference was hosted by Luthern Social Services of San Antonio, Texas, an agency which supports open records and open adoption. The 1983 national conference will be held May 19-22 in Columbus, Ohio at the Hilton Inn East.

Do Birthparents Really Care...Forever?

The membership of Concerned United Birthparents would respond to that question with a resounding YES. CUB was born in 1976 in S.E. Massachusetts to an attractive young woman who called herself Lenore Hatch. Imagine the *real* Lee Campbell using an alias. Society had done its job well. Lee continued to use her alias until early in 1977 when she felt strong enough to let go of the mask. So Lenore "hatched" CUB, but Lee has kept it growing and thriving. It has gone from its' infant stage to a full-grown organization in a relatively short period of time.

I had the privilege of starting the first local branch of CUB in July of 1977 in southern New Jersey. In 1979 Lee appointed me Branch Administrator, responsible for setting up branches around the country and helping new leaders get started. In 1981, in order to provide interaction on a more personal basis and since so many new branches were being added, a regional system was developed and six regional co-ordinators assumed leadership roles to handle the growing demand. Lee's three appearances on Donahue gave CUB the boost it needed and thousands responded.

CUB has a pamphlet available that answers such questions as "What is CUB's position on the current controversy over sealed records? Don't some adoptive parents view CUB as a threat? Don't most birthparents want to be anonymous?

What are the obstacles impeding relationships among those involved in adoptions? Do you have a solution for the teenage pregnancy epidemic? Is CUB against adoption? What kind of adoption system would CUB support? Are there places where open placements are being arranged?" To order this very informative booklet, send $1.00 and a legal sized, self-addressed stamped envelope to CUB, Box 573, Milford, Massachusetts 01757.

CUB also has some interesting statistics developing. The early research deals with the average age of the CUB member, the amount of time lapsed since surrender, the adoption facilitator, the reason for surrender, whether the member is in search or not, data concerning marriage, info about the other birthparent, how many subsequent children, etc. For instance, the early research shows that a substantial number of birthparents never had subsequent children. Another interesting statistic is how many birthmothers married the birthfather. CUB will be continuing with in-depth research studies concerning the effects of birthparenthood.

Since CUB believes that prevention is as important as cure, the Dover, New Hampshire office offers young parents and other "at risk" youths the self-sufficiency and esteem building opportunity of Business Education Training. It's called the B.E.T. on Youth Program.

Presently pregnant teens are linked with "been there" members as part of the CUB Sister Program, ensuring disclosure of all alternatives and free choice.

With the preceding background of the adoption movement, you can see how this phenomenon has grown over the past ten years. The tide is becoming more powerful each day and nothing can stop its flow. The pioneers of the last decade have broken ground and laid the foundation. The next decade will see many changes in adoption.

The adoption movement was created in response to a need; the need to know. Those who have this need sometimes find the first step the most difficult one to take. Following are some ideas that may encourage you to get started on your journey.

Finding the Needle in the Haystack

The very first thing you need to do is to decide once and for all that you're going to do it and then DO. The biggest mistake many people make is to put off their search. So many have had regrets because they waited too long to begin. Instead of looking into the face of the one they were searching, they found only a cold grave.

Another reason for starting immediately is the fact that some searches take several years to complete. Waiting could destroy possible leads that are available at the present time, but may not be a month or year from now. So don't put it off once you're decided that it's what you want to do.

Though you may not be close enough to attend a local group meeting, you can be in touch with them by mail. Remember that you are not alone. There are at least 5 million adoptees in this country; therefore there are 10 million adoptive parents and 10 million birthparents. Add to those figures the number of siblings on each side and you realize that adoption directly affects almost 60 million people. Therefore, through the exchange of ideas and information, you will have greater success in being able to achieve your goal - which is to find! It will also help you emotionally as you interact with others who have "walked in your shoes." So don't try to go it alone - because you're not alone.

Keep in mind when searching for someone that there

is no easy, simple, or fast way of finding a person. There could be, but usually there isn't. There are times when I wish it were possible to hand someone the information on a silver platter - but that's not reality. The fact is that most searches involve time, money and perserverance. The point is not to give up. When you get to the end of your rope, remember that's the time to tie a knot and hang on! Don't quit - something will break.

Each search is different. What works for one may not work for another. But YOU are the one who has the greatest stake in your search. That's why it's so important for YOU to do most of the legwork yourself. You are your own best investigator. No one else will put quite as much effort into your search as YOU. And you may spend a lot of money paying someone else to do it who may not be able to turn up anything. I would suggest paying *only* when you are *guaranteed* accurate information and only then if the fee seems reasonable. Be cautious. People have been extorted large sums of money for little information and still had to do a search.

Don't be intimidated by "professionals". Those of us in the adoption triangle have suffered all kinds of hang-ups - from the "good" adoptee who doesn't want to make waves to the "guilt-ridden" birthmother who is still paying for her sin. We seem to be easily intimidated by those in authority who seem to have control over our lives and the information we so desperately need. We are called "selfish, inconsiderate, ungrateful", etc. Adoptees are told "If your mother really wanted you, she would have kept you." Birthparents are told "You made your decision - you gave up all your rights." These kinds of comments and charges can put a person back into the closet quicker than anything else. Don't allow it. Take charge of your life. You have a right to your feelings and you know that those charges are not true! Strive to attain greater self-confidence and self-esteem. They will be your greatest assets as you pursue your goal.

Keep records as you begin your search by keeping

copies of every letter you send, noting each phone call, who you spoke to, what the conversation entailed, etc. Don't trust these things to memory - too often it fails us. When an idea comes to mind, jot it down. Don't pass over *any* information. Something that seems very minor or unimportant could be the very thing to "break your case".

Genealogy research has been around for a long time, but it's recently become a popular pasttime for many. When calling places for information, do not mention adoption - it could work against you. Remember, that we are still fighting against a social prejudice. You are simply doing genealogy research - which is true.

Learn how to search through deeds, land records, tax lists, marriage and divorce records, and birth and death indexes. These are available to the public in *most* states, though not all.

Finally, in dealing with agencies, beware of false or misleading information. They have been known to send searchers "barking up the wrong tree!"

Adoptees and birthparents are searching in greater numbers and being successful in those searches; in many cases, with the support of adoptive parents. If you are now "in search", pursue it through to completion.

Those of us who have been in the movement for some time have discovered that it's difficult for an individual to be actively involved in "the cause" while "in search". We understand that. But we do sincerely hope that after you've found, you will stay around long enough to aid someone else. We also invite you to join our AWARENESS PROJECT.

THE AWARENESS PROJECT (What you can do to help)

There are many things you can do, and a good place to start is by supporting PROJECT AWARENESS*. The Awareness Project reflects a direct desire in those who make up both the immediate adoption trinity and the peripheral circle. It will serve to educate both movement people and uninvolved people. It will help alleviate the fear and secrecy we so despise. It will offer alternatives in thought, action and ideas.

What is awareness. Websters Dictionary says "aware implies having knowledge of something through alertness in observing or in interpreting what one sees, hears, feels, etc."

To make people more aware of the inequalities and inhumanities that take place within adoption, we must, therefore, cause them to be alert. How? That is what the Project is all about. Discovering new and different ways to call attention to the plight of adoptees, birthparents, and adoptive parents as we grow to encompass the vast change that is taking place in our midst.

Each of us is responsible for doing our part. Adoption is not removed from anyone. When an adoptee must spend years of his/her life looking and fighting for a simple piece of information, they are not free to hold their full place of responsibility in society; when a birthparent harbors a silent longing and a multitude of unexpressed love; when an adoptive parent gulps in fear that they may one day face another reality. . .another parent, they too are functioning at partial fulfillment. What a better world is in store when the seals and secrecy are lifted!

Those that maintain vigilance over adoption cannot possibly have the spectrum of information at their disposal. It is not possible to make them hear, see or feel, but we can offer alternatives. We can give effort to spreading ideas, facts, feelings and experiences.

We can tell our neighbor that there is a deep hurt inside because twenty years ago we gave up a child. We can admit that we DO want to know those mythical folks who gave us life. There is plenty that we CAN do. Each time we express our feelings or share experiences, we spread the word. The next time that person hears the term adoption, they may think a bit differently about it.

Give of yourself. Talk openly. Each time you share, the natural law of pyramiding will take over. One person will go on to tell another and another and another. YOU can make the difference. If you tell five people, you've now reached twenty-five. If it goes on and each of them tells five people. . .now it's one hundred and twenty-five and on and on. Remember that the Lord spread His word through twelve committed men.

What does Awareness mean? For us it means open records, open adoption, reunions, and so much more! For movement groups, 'adopting' (excuse the pun) this project as a workable program will give form to all kinds of tangible ideas. For the individual, it means acknowledging that there is something you can do. No one is alone in this movement. We are all friends bound by a common foundation and goal. Do you feel a little more aware now? If you do. . . .the project works! Go out and share it!

(Excerpt from Triad Options, 1979)

SECTION VI

HIS BANNER OVER ME IS LOVE

"He who has ears let him hear." Matt. 11:15

Jesus

THE SUPREME SACRIFICE

God, something occurred to me recently as I was thinking about the child I had to surrender years ago. I recall that you, too, gave up Your child. I've studied in your Word how painful that was and what a great sacrifice - to give up Your Son. Apparently there was no other way or You would have found it.[1]

You know, Lord, I also gave up my child. There was no other way either. But I am comforted in knowing that You have walked in my footsteps and understand my heartache.

But You were reconciled with Your Son, Lord. They tell me I have no right to be reconciled with mine. Since Your Son was brought into the world for the express purpose of reconciliation[2] - could it be that my child might accomplish that same end - bringing together two sets of parents, siblings and other extended family members who love him?

Wasn't that Your ultimate goal when You made the decision to make the supreme sacrifice[3] - to reconcile us to one another, to teach us how to love and thereby draw us closer to You?

Lord, if those of us who are intimately involved in adoption can accomplish that goal, then the supreme sacrifice will not have been in vain - neither Yours nor mine.

An Aching Birthmother

[1] Isaiah 53   [2] 2 Corinthians 5:19   [3] John 1:29

The Trinity and the Triangle

I am continually astonished how much of our adoption "lingo" is like that of the scriptures, as well as the many analogies that can be drawn. Some examples follow:

The words "chosen" and "rejected" are used repeatedly. The inferences are that the Jews were the "chosen" people, but they "rejected" the Messiah and therefore the gentiles were grafted in (adopted) making them the "chosen" sons of God by way of adoption. In Exodus 4:22, the Lord is talking to Moses and telling him to tell Pharaoh that "Israel is my son, even my *firstborn*." The Bible goes on to explain how the Israelites became scattered - Ezek. 34:6 "*My sheep* wandered through all the mountains and upon every high hill; yes, my flock was scattered upon all the face of the earth." But then it goes on to point out how God's plan for His people was and still is reconciliation when He said, "Behold, I even I, will both search *my sheep* and seek them out." (Ezek. 34:11)

Jesus Christ, the promised Messiah, became a stumbling block to the Jewish people. He paved the way for them to enjoy the fruit of salvation, which was something they were unable to do on their own. Could it be that birthparents are stumbling blocks to adoptive parents - since the birthparent made possible what was otherwise impossible? The Jews could not save themselves (nor can any of us, which is why we all need a Savior) - nor can an infertile parent enjoy of benefits of parenting apart from the woman who gives birth and is willing to sacrifice a part of herself.

Another similar term used is the word "intermediary". Over and over again Jesus is referred to as the "intermediary" - the only way to the Father. How many of us have found the one person who became our "intermediary", and thereby paved the way for us to meet that special person we had been seeking?

The Trinity is another good analogy. Those of us raised in the Christian faith are familiar with the concept. The Trinity consists of three persons in one - the Father, Son, and Holy Spirit. These three make up what is known as the Godhead. My own personal understanding of that truth is that those three persons actually have three separate roles while being one complete unit.

How alike is the adoption triangle! We are three separate parts, but certainly one unit - a unit intricately knit into one whole. The birthparents have given their heredity; the adoptive parents have provided the environment; and finally, the adoptee, benefiting from both, become their own unique person.

Each fulfills their role as best they can - one does not think their position in the triangle of any more importance than the other. Each realizes and understands that the other does not negate nor detract from their own particular role.

Throughout scripture, the Father, Son and Holy Spirit are always depicted as giving glory to one another. What an example for us in the Triangle! We have been bound together. We may not even understand why, but we do know that we need not fear one another. It is His love that casts out fear (I John 4:18). Nor has He given us a spirit of fear, but of power and love (II Tim. 1:7). Here are some scriptural references that may help bring about a greater understanding as we apply them to our adoption experience.

In emphasizing the everlasting presence and power of God we are told in Psalms 139 that we are wondrously created and that God knew all that was going on in the process. That shows us the omniscience and omnipresence of God in the marvelous processes of creation and procreation. In verse 13 and 14, it states. . ."thou has covered me in my mother's womb. I will praise you for I am fearfully and wonderfully made." The following verses go on to show that none of us are here by accident for it says, "My substance was not hid from you when I was made in secret. . .Your eyes did see my substance while still imperfect, and in your book all my members were written which in continuance were fashioned when as yet there was none of them."

Isaiah 44:24 states, "Thus said the Lord your Redeemer and He that formed you from the womb; I am the Lord that maketh all things". In Isaiah 45:15 the question is being posed, "Can a woman forget her sucking child that she should not have compassion on the son of her womb?" The inference, of course, is that it's very unlikely that any mother ever forgets the child of her womb! However, it goes on to state, "though they may forget, yet will I not forget you. . .I have graven you upon the palms of my hands."

Parables of Reconciliation

Reconciliation permeates the scriptures. From Moses longing for his kin to Joseph being reunited with his brothers who had sold him into salvery; from the parable of the lost sheep to the parable of the lost coin and the return of the prodigal son; from the angels in heaven rejoicing over one returning soul - to the unity of the trinity.

The following parables were presented by Jesus, particularly for the sake of the Pharisees who looked upon "sinners" with contempt. They illustrate God's concern for the lost, but also show Pharisees that they, indeed, are the ones in greatest need.

Luke 15:4 - A shepherd counted his sheep at the close of each day to make sure none had strayed. If one was missing, he searched for it immediately. Not only did he track down the sheep, but he also made direct contact with it. In the scripture, the phrase "go after" connotes persistence and success. When he found it, he calls together his friends and neighbors and says "Rejoice with me; for I have found *my* sheep which was lost.

Luke 15:8 - Since coins were scarcer in Palestine than they are in modern civilization, they represented the savings of many years. In this parable we see that a woman is about to sweep her house clean in order to find one lost coin - though she had nine others. All her energies are put into the search. She lights a candle for the express purpose of having the light shine in order for her to find. The broom used for other purposes now sweeps only to find the missing coin. Her two eyes look for nothing else. Her candle, her broom, her eyesight, her body limbs, her faculties of mind are all employed in searching for the lost treasure.

Luke 15:11 - The next parable popularly known as the Prodigal Son could more aptly be called The Father's Open Arms. Though many years had separated them and the son was no longer a part of the family circle, the father was constantly watching for the return of his boy. We are told that when the father saw him coming, he reserved the best robe (always reserved for an honored guest) and a ring (which marked the position of sonship). A feast was immediately held. The fatted calf spoken of was the animal held in readiness for a special occasion. The return of his son was the cause for a major celebration. The reaction of the son who had been with him was one of jealousy and disgust. He was angry over what he regarded as an injustice when he expressed,, "All these many years have I served you!" The language implies self-righteousness, self-pity, and an inward alienation from his father. The father then reminds him that he has been ever with him, and all that he has is his - "but this your brother was dead, and is alive again; and was lost and is found."

The preceding parables seem to express that God is intently interested in reconciliations - not only spiritual reconciliation, but physical reconciliation as well.

Who Can Judge?
John 8:1-11 - When the woman taken in adultery was brought before Jesus by the scribes and Pharisees, he turned the searchlight on their own self-righteousness, rather than

upon the victim. On more than one occasion, in an effort to correct hypocrisy, He said that even harlots would enter the kingdom before those whose works appeared more pious than they actually were (Matt. 21:31).

John 4:7-42 - "God is a spirit and they that worship him must worship him in spirit and truth." This message was given to the Woman of Samaria by Jesus. She was a woman who the Bible says had five husbands. Isn't it quite a paradox that this woman would be chosen to receive his teaching that "God is a spirit." As they stood by the well that day, He told her of living water. He had asked for water which was temporal, but He had, in turn, given her the eternal gift of spiritual fountains for the soul. That fountain is God, Himself, who must be worshipped in spirit and truth, by saint and sinner alike. In fact, the sinner may draw closer to Him more quickly than the self-satisfied, righteous person who has a tendency to look down on those he considers less righteous than himself.

This story confirms the belief that God is no respector of persons and that Jesus came to show the inner meaning of spirituality. Spiritual refreshment comes into the soul after an encounter with Him. How comforting it is to know that there is such a fountain of living water to refresh those of us who suffer from the injustices of a system that continues to separate and deny individuals their God-given right to roots - their birthright.

Genealogy in the Bible

Genealogy has been given a prominent place in the Bible. One does not have to look very far before finding lots of begats: Abraham begat Isaac, Isaac begat Jacob, and so on and so on. This would seem to indicate that much of a person's identity is closely related to the families from which he or she is descended.

Called to be a Deliverer

Jochebed, mother of Moses, gained her strength from her faith in things unseen. At the time she gave birth to Moses, the Pharoah had issued an edict to midwives to kill all Hebrew male children at birth. Moses had a natural birth, but the fact that he survived and grew up when all male Hebrew children were being destroyed is noteworthy.

How Jochebed managed to save her son during the first three months of Moses' life is not recorded. But after he became three months old, she decided upon a plan of leaving her baby in a handmade ark.

With the help of her daughter, Miriam, she laid her baby among the papyrus reeds near the river's bank and left Miriam to watch over him. Jochebed knew that Pharoah's daughter was accustomed to come down and bathe at this spot. (Today this is called abandonment, but notice how this mother is *planning* her child's placement).

Pharoah's daughter did appear with her maidens and came upon the ark. She heard the whimpering child, and said "This is one of the Hebrews' children." (Exod. 2:6)

Young Miriam, standing close by said, "Shall I go and call a nurse of the Hebrew women, that she may nurse the child for you? (Exod. 2:7,8) And Pharoah's daughter said to her, Go." (Exod. 2:8)

So it was that Jochebed received the joyful news that

she could nurse her own child. Though Moses was soon adopted by Pharaoh's daughter, it was his own mother who would watch over him as a child. It was Jochebed who instilled in him a belief in God. It was she who imparted to him the sacred traditions of Israel and who told him of the divine promise to Abraham and his decendants that they would become a great nation.

And yet this unassuming Levite mother could rejoice that her son Moses, as the adopted son of the princess, did receive the best education available in a king's palace and would later have the privilege of an education of the highest order. What other Hebrew son could be so blessed. What other mother could know such inward joy? (Certainly an example for us today of an open adoption and the benefits to all.)

In later years Moses would remember his mother's God and the faith she had in Him. He would remain a Hebrew through all the years of his life. The scripture tells us that when He became a man, he went out among his own brethern and lifted their burden. He became their deliverer. He had been called to set his people free. He was not a willing subject. In fact, he made all kinds of excuses as to why he was not the man for the job. First he questioned God by saying, "Who am I, that I should go to Pharaoh and that I should bring forth the children of Israel out of Egypt?" And each time the Lord answered him, he had another excuse ready. He replied that they wouldn't believe him; then he said that he was not eloquent and his speech was slow. The Lord replied, "Who has made man's mouth or who made the dumb, or deaf, or the seeing or the blind? Have not I the Lord? Go therefore and I will teach you what you should say." (Ex. 4:11)

As the story progresses, we see that Moses gains more and more courage and finally takes his proper place as leader.

I share the above to draw an analogy to those of us in the adoption movement. Moses' people were in physical bondage. Our people are in mental bondage. We need more spokespersons to speak on behalf of adoptees, birthparents, adoptive parents and siblings, who are being kept in bondage by the "taskmasters" (the system, the court, the agency, etc). Along with many others, I have accepted the challenge, but not without giving many of the same excuses that Moses gave. With the support of family and friends, I've gained more and more courage and am now dedicated to this challenge.

When you've been set free by a completed search, have settled your "adoption experience", or just believe in basic rights, shouldn't it be your privilege, your honor and your duty to help someone else become free? Will you join me in this challenge - the challenge to set our people free? If your answer is yes, then will you also have a share in my dream?

My dream is to create a place for searchers to come and spend as much time as they need learning the "how to" of search and search techniques. There would be every kind of research material available at their fingertips.

It would be a place for girls and women with "untimely" pregnancies to come and find solace, without pressure, while examining their alternatives.

It would be a place for perspective adoptive parents to learn more about open adoption and consider it as a viable choice for themselves, after dealing with their infertility.

It would be a place for professionals to come to study the concepts, the theories, and finally the "hands on" experience of open adoption.

It would be a place where seminars and workshops would be held on a regular basis, both in-house and around the country. They would deal with all aspects of loss and separation.

Yes, it would be a place of learning and it will be called Adoption Educational Institute for Openness and Understanding (AEIOU). It would be a clearinghouse for open adoptions.

If you believe we can create such a place, if you believe it would be a worthwhile project, and if you think you have something to offer by way of facilities, services, or just ideas as to establishing, supporting, and maintaining such an operation, please write and let me know.

Your letters, resumes and contributions will become part of the Adoption Educational Institute Foundation as we look to the future and consider the feasibility of such a facility.

Maybe together we can turn this dream into reality so that the day will come when no one will have to go "in search", because openness will be the law of the land.

Is it possible?

Write to me in care of:

A.E.I.
P. O. Box 532
Manasquan, New Jersey 08736

In Conclusion:

If you are a Christian, but are still on the fence concerning this issue, may I remind you that God gave us the work of reconciliation (II Cor. 5:18). Through this movement, we have great opportunities to do that work He's called us to do - by reuniting loved ones separated from birth. Won't you, too, commit yourself to this task?

If you are not a Christian, I would like to share with you my deep belief that the greatest reunion and reconciliation is still taking place at the foot of the cross. And when you've been reconciled to your Maker, you'll know within your spirit that reconciliation is what He deserves for all His children.

Postscript - The Ultimate Reunion

June 29, 1982, marked another milestone in my emotional healing. That was the day I met with the birthfather for the first time in twenty-eight years. It was one of the most healing experiences, and I only regret that it didn't occur sooner.

The AAC conference of 1981 had brought many unresolved feelings to the surface that I didn't even realize I had. Though I'd been active in the movement for five years, I still had not begun to deal on an emotional level. The 1982 conference awakened those feelings even more, which began a process within me.

The stark reality that I would never know my daughter as a child suddenly surfaced as I listened to a musical tape and watched correlated slides of young children. Yes, I knew intellectually that those years were gone forever, but the emotional impact struck like a ton of bricks as a flood of tears was released that day.

Painful? Yes. But healing is well on its way. Like physical healing, emotional healing takes longer for some of us than for others. There will always be a scar, but a scar doesn't hurt. The scar is the reminder of the pain once suffered.

A few days following the conference, I had contact with the birthfather. When I expressed my need to discuss feelings concerning the manner in which our relationship ended, he agreed to meet with me. At the same time, we made arrangements for him to meet his daughter.

We met for lunch and spent several hours discussing the past and present. He shared how, over the years, he had justified his actions by telling himself "There wasn't anything you could have done for her. You were only fifteen." But then he went on, "There was something I could have done, but I was a coward. I could have given you emotional support. I could have 'been there' for you and I wasn't. All I can say is - I'm sorry." I guess "I'm sorry" is what I needed to hear because twenty-eight years of hurt melted away. Ridiculous, you say. Maybe. All I know is that the burden I had carried for those twenty-eight years was lifted when I heard him speak those few little words.

We then drove to Cindy's home where she and her birthfather greeted one another with a hug. I then took my "adopted" grandson for a ride so Cindy and her birthfather could spend some time alone. When I returned, the three of us spent a few more hours sharing ourselves and our lives with one another. I was amazed at how comfortable it felt.

I'm sure I am speaking on behalf of all of us when I say that there are no words to describe the feeling of wholeness that comes from such an encounter. Our smiling faces, shining forth from the pictures we took, give a glowing memory of that day in June when the three of us came together for a healing reunion. Mission accomplished!

The following poem was written by my Grandfather, Donald F. Saxton. He wrote it in 1964 following the death of my Grandmother. I believe it shows the depth of longing we all have to be reunited with loved ones from whom we've become separated - whether that separation is caused by adoption, divorce, or death. And it also speaks of HOPE - "For now we see through a glass darkly, but then we will know even as we are known when we see Him face to face." II Cor. 13:12.

Our Reunion

Sometimes I think life isn't fair
Seems like I did not get my share
But when the sum is up dear friend
We borrowed more than we could lend.

Now if we try to pay it back
I'm sure a million times we'll lack
Because the price was set you see
On bended knee and CALVARY.

He did it Oh with love so great
To leave behind all sin and hate
For GOD is good and GOD is love
That's why He made the heaven above.
My heart is sad, my loss so great
Until I think of the Pearly gate
Which she has entered like a dream
For her reward of life supreme.

Now this I know, I knew her well
The day or date I can't foretell
But this I know, that she will wait
Just near the shining Pearly gate.

I'll grasp her arm as she will mine
We will not even need a sign
She'll know me when I say Dear Heart
Now we'll never have to part.

We'll start our walk up Jesus Lane
We'll know it by the great refrains
And when we come within the scope
To climax all our faith and hope -
We'll lay ourselves down at His feet
And say to him, Dear Jesus Sweet
We don't deserve to see your face
Save only by THY Matchless Grace.

Then He will say to us once more
Arise and walk the Golden Shore
I paid the price by sincere love
Enjoy forever these skies above.

Then around the shore we'll walk some more
To greet the loved ones gone before
And then return to JESUS Lane
To be a Part of the Great refrain.

Grandpa was reunited with her on August 27, 1979.

Adoption Groups

There are over 300 local search and support groups across the country. When writing to any of the following national organizations and/or individuals, please be sure to include a self-addressed stamped envelope if you would like a reply. Writing to one of these groups will help you to tie into a local group in your area.

National Organizations

American Adoption
  Congress (AAC)
P. O. Box 23641
Washington, DC 20024

Adoption Triangle
  Ministry (ATM)
P. O. Box 156
Oaklyn, NJ 08107

Adoption Consultants, Inc.
9320 S.W. 170th Street
Miami, FL 33157

Adoptive Parents for Open
  Records
9 Marjorie Drive
Hackettstown, NJ 07840

ALMA
P. O. Box 154
Washington Bridge Station
New York, NY 10033

Concerned United
  Birthparents (CUB)
P. O. Box 573
Milford, MA 01757

Independent Search
   Consultants
P. O. Box 10192
Costa Mesa, CA 92627

Parent Finders
1408 W. 45th Avenue
Vancouver, B.C.
Canada V6M 2H1

International Soundex
   Reunion Registry (ISRR)
P. O. Box 2312
Carson City, NV 89702

Post Adoption Center for
   Education and Research
   (PACER)
860 Bryant Street
Palo Alto, CA 94301

Open Arms
P. O. Box 1522
North Platte, NE 69101

Triadoption Library
7571 Westminster Avenue
Westminster, CA 92683

Orphan Voyage
Cedaredge, CO 81413

ISRR Representatives

Diana E. Brown
ISRR Eastern Rep.
5288 Winter's Chapel Road
Doraville, GA 30360

June Tanner
ISRR Central Rep.
6602 Manchester
Raytown, MO 64133

Sally File
ISRR Western Rep.
13101 Blackstone NE
Albuquerque, NM 87111

CUB Sister Program

Charleen Justice, Coordinator
Box A292
Deptford, NJ 08096

ATM Representatives

Joan Arnette
Rt. 1, Box 159A
Cameron, WI 54822

Pat Berkram
Star Rt.
Cut Bank, MT 59427

David Bryant
37 E. Walnut Avenue
Merchantville, NJ 08109

Juanita Currie
1645 5th Place NW
Birmingham, AL 35215

Debbie Davis
7500 Cogswell Road
Romulus, MI 48174

Joan Dexheimer
Box 250B06
Los Angeles, CA 90025

Carol Gustavson
9 Marjorie Drive
Hackettstown, NJ 07840

Tiffany Johnson
Rt. 1, Box 743
Lakeside, AZ 85929

Colleen Martin
1234 Oak Road
Manasquan, NJ 08736

Marsha Smith
6512 Hudson Avenue
Norfolk, VA 23502

Laurel Sparf
204 Jersey Avenue
Normal, IL 61761

Jo Anne Swanson
Box 121
L'Anse, MI 49945

Pat Tulles
965 E. 14th Street
Idaho Falls, ID 83401

Carole Vaile
Braemoor Farm, RR No. 6
Renfrew, Ontario K7V 3Z9

Gloria Veillon
134 Memory Lane
Lafayette, LA 70506

Sara Vick - San Francisco Bay Area
c/o Headquarters, Box 156
Oaklyn, NJ 08107

Susan Wallace
Box 526
New Castle, DE 19720

Darlene Webster
130 Water Oak Way
Oldsmar, FL 33557

ATM Representatives

(continued)

Susan Secchi
2159 Lansill Road
Lexington, KY 40504

Terry West
616 ElDorado Parkway
Cape Coral, FL 33904

Jana Shedlock
7105 Shooresin Circle
Anchorage, Alaska 99504

Robin Wilson
11 Sweetbriar Lane
Chapel Hill, NC 27514

Julie Bissey
P. O. Box 115
Haddon Heights, NJ 08035

American Adoption Congress Regional Directors

Region 1
CT, ME, MA, NH, RI, VT

Jo & Peter Devlin
34 Pleasant Street
Stoneham, MA 02180

Region 2
DE, MD, NJ, NY, PA, VA, DC

Jane Reifler
5502 S. Bend Road
Baltimore, MD 21209

Region 3
AL, FL, GA, MS, NC, SC, TN

Pam Lawrence
490 W. New York Avenue
Orange City, FL 32753

Region 4
AR, LA, TX

Gloria Veillon
Box 3932
Lafayette, LA 70502

Region 5
IN, KY, MI, OH, WV

Penny Harris
6912 Waltham NW
Canton, OH 44708

Region 6
CO, IA, KS, MO, NE, OK

Elizabeth Scott
Rt. 2, Oak Crest Estates
Rogersville, MO 65742

Region 7
IL, MN, ND, SD, WI

Linda Lincoln
66 E. Cedar
Chicago, IL 60611

Region 8
AK, ID, MT, OR, WA, WY

Emmie Allen
Box 1332
Beaverton, OR 97075

Region 9
AZ, CA, HI, NV, NM, UT

Pat Sanders
20111 Riverside
Santa Ana, CA 92707

Region 10
Canadian Providences

Mary Jane Brinkos
120 Eglinton Ave. East
Toronto, Ontario M4P 1E2

Sandy Musser is available for speaking engagements.

Bulk copies of this book are available at a discount.

For information concerning the above, contact:

Steve Zimmerman
(609) 667-0291

or write

Jan Publications
Box 156
Oaklyn, NJ 08107